GEORGES JACQUES DANTON

GEORGES JACQUES DANTON

Frank Dwyer

CHELSEA HOUSE PUBLISHERS
NEW YORK
NEW HAVEN   PHILADELPHIA

EDITOR-IN-CHIEF: Nancy Toff
EXECUTIVE EDITOR: Remmel T. Nunn
MANAGING EDITOR: Karyn Gullen Browne
COPY CHIEF: Perry Scott King
ART DIRECTOR: Giannella Garrett
PICTURE EDITOR: Elizabeth Terhune

Staff for GEORGES JACQUES DANTON:

SENIOR EDITOR: John W. Selfridge
ASSISTANT EDITORS: Maria Behan, Pierre Hauser, Kathleen McDermott, Bert Yaeger
COPY EDITORS: Gillian Bucky, Sean Dolan
DESIGN ASSISTANT: Jill Goldreyer
PICTURE RESEARCH: Juliette Dickstein
LAYOUT: David Murray
PRODUCTION COORDINATOR: Alma Rodriguez
COVER ILLUSTRATION: Richard Martin

CREATIVE DIRECTOR: Harold Steinberg

Copyright © 1987 by Chelsea House Publishers, a division of
Chelsea House Educational Communications, Inc. All rights reserved.
Printed and bound in the United States of America.

Frontispiece courtesy of The Bettmann Archive

3 5 7 9 8 6 4 2

Library of Congress Cataloging in Publication Data

Dwyer, Frank. DANTON

(World leaders past & present)
Bibliography: p.
Includes index.
1. Danton, Georges Jacques, 1759–1794—Juvenile
literature. 2. Revolutionists—France—Biography—Juvenile
literature. 3. France—History—Revolution, 1789–1794—
Juvenile literature. I. Title. II. Series.
DC146.D2D88   1987   944.04′092′4 [B]   86-29930

ISBN 0-87754-519-7

Contents

"On Leadership," Arthur M. Schlesinger, jr. 7

1. "It's Worth a Look" 13
2. The Republican 19
3. Monsieur d'Anton 27
4. The King of the Cordeliers 37
5. Rivals and a Rising Star 47
6. Two Fugitives 57
7. The King of the Jacobins 63
8. Savior of France................................... 73
9. The Wars of the Deputies 83
10. "My Address Will Soon Be Nowhere"................. 95

Further Reading................................... 108
Chronology....................................... 109
Index.. 110

CHELSEA HOUSE PUBLISHERS

WORLD LEADERS PAST & PRESENT

ADENAUER
ALEXANDER THE GREAT
MARC ANTONY
KING ARTHUR
ATATÜRK
ATTLEE
BEGIN
BEN-GURION
BISMARCK
LÉON BLUM
BOLÍVAR
CESARE BORGIA
BRANDT
BREZHNEV
CAESAR
CALVIN
CASTRO
CATHERINE THE GREAT
CHARLEMAGNE
CHIANG KAI-SHEK
CHURCHILL
CLEMENCEAU
CLEOPATRA
CORTÉS
CROMWELL
DANTON
DE GAULLE
DE VALERA
DISRAELI
EISENHOWER
ELEANOR OF AQUITAINE
QUEEN ELIZABETH I
FERDINAND AND ISABELLA
FRANCO

FREDERICK THE GREAT
INDIRA GANDHI
MOHANDAS GANDHI
GARIBALDI
GENGHIS KHAN
GLADSTONE
GORBACHEV
HAMMARSKJÖLD
HENRY VIII
HENRY OF NAVARRE
HINDENBURG
HITLER
HO CHI MINH
HUSSEIN
IVAN THE TERRIBLE
ANDREW JACKSON
JEFFERSON
JOAN OF ARC
POPE JOHN XXIII
LYNDON JOHNSON
JUÁREZ
JOHN F. KENNEDY
KENYATTA
KHOMEINI
KHRUSHCHEV
MARTIN LUTHER KING, JR.
KISSINGER
LENIN
LINCOLN
LLOYD GEORGE
LOUIS XIV
LUTHER
JUDAS MACCABEUS
MAO ZEDONG

MARY, QUEEN OF SCOTS
GOLDA MEIR
METTERNICH
MUSSOLINI
NAPOLEON
NASSER
NEHRU
NERO
NICHOLAS II
NIXON
NKRUMAH
PERICLES
PERÓN
QADDAFI
ROBESPIERRE
ELEANOR ROOSEVELT
FRANKLIN D. ROOSEVELT
THEODORE ROOSEVELT
SADAT
STALIN
SUN YAT-SEN
TAMERLANE
THATCHER
TITO
TROTSKY
TRUDEAU
TRUMAN
VICTORIA
WASHINGTON
WEIZMANN
WOODROW WILSON
XERXES
ZHOU ENLAI

ON LEADERSHIP
Arthur M. Schlesinger, jr.

LEADERSHIP, it may be said, is really what makes the world go round. Love no doubt smooths the passage; but love is a private transaction between consenting adults. Leadership is a public transaction with history. The idea of leadership affirms the capacity of individuals to move, inspire, and mobilize masses of people so that they act together in pursuit of an end. Sometimes leadership serves good purposes, sometimes bad; but whether the end is benign or evil, great leaders are those men and women who leave their personal stamp on history.

Now, the very concept of leadership implies the proposition that individuals can make a difference. This proposition has never been universally accepted. From classical times to the present day, eminent thinkers have regarded individuals as no more than the agents and pawns of larger forces, whether the gods and goddesses of the ancient world or, in the modern era, race, class, nation, the dialectic, the will of the people, the spirit of the times, history itself. Against such forces, the individual dwindles into insignificance.

So contends the thesis of historical determinism. Tolstoy's great novel *War and Peace* offers a famous statement of the case. Why, Tolstoy asked, did millions of men in the Napoleonic wars, denying their human feelings and their common sense, move back and forth across Europe slaughtering their fellows? "The war," Tolstoy answered, "was bound to happen simply because it was bound to happen." All prior history predetermined it. As for leaders, they, Tolstoy said, "are but the labels that serve to give a name to an end and, like labels, they have the least possible connection with the event." The greater the leader, "the more conspicuous the inevitability and the predestination of every act he commits." The leader, said Tolstoy, is "the slave of history."

Determinism takes many forms. Marxism is the determinism of class. Nazism the determinism of race. But the idea of men and women as the slaves of history runs athwart the deepest human instincts. Rigid determinism abolishes the idea of human freedom—

the assumption of free choice that underlies every move we make, every word we speak, every thought we think. It abolishes the idea of human responsibility, since it is manifestly unfair to reward or punish people for actions that are by definition beyond their control. No one can live consistently by any deterministic creed. The Marxist states prove this themselves by their extreme susceptibility to the cult of leadership.

More than that, history refutes the idea that individuals make no difference. In December 1931 a British politician crossing Park Avenue in New York City between 76th and 77th Streets around 10:30 P.M. looked in the wrong direction and was knocked down by an automobile—a moment, he later recalled, of a man aghast, a world aglare: "I do not understand why I was not broken like an eggshell or squashed like a gooseberry." Fourteen months later an American politician, sitting in an open car in Miami, Florida, was fired on by an assassin; the man beside him was hit. Those who believe that individuals make no difference to history might well ponder whether the next two decades would have been the same had Mario Constasino's car killed Winston Churchill in 1931 and Giuseppe Zangara's bullet killed Franklin Roosevelt in 1933. Suppose, in addition, that Adolf Hitler had been killed in the street fighting during the Munich *Putsch* of 1923 and that Lenin had died of typhus during World War I. What would the 20th century be like now?

For better or for worse, individuals do make a difference. "The notion that a people can run itself and its affairs anonymously," wrote the philosopher William James, "is now well known to be the silliest of absurdities. Mankind does nothing save through initiatives on the part of inventors, great or small, and imitation by the rest of us—these are the sole factors in human progress. Individuals of genius show the way, and set the patterns, which common people then adopt and follow."

Leadership, James suggests, means leadership in thought as well as in action. In the long run, leaders in thought may well make the greater difference to the world. But, as Woodrow Wilson once said, "Those only are leaders of men, in the general eye, who lead in action. . . . It is at their hands that new thought gets its translation into the crude language of deeds." Leaders in thought often invent in solitude and obscurity, leaving to later generations the tasks of imitation. Leaders in action—the leaders portrayed in this series—have to be effective in their own time.

And they cannot be effective by themselves. They must act in response to the rhythms of their age. Their genius must be adapted, in a phrase of William James's, "to the receptivities of the moment." Leaders are useless without followers. "There goes the mob," said the French politician hearing a clamor in the streets. "I am their leader. I must follow them." Great leaders turn the inchoate emotions of the mob to purposes of their own. They seize on the opportunities of their time, the hopes, fears, frustrations, crises, potentialities. They succeed when events have prepared the way for them, when the community is awaiting to be aroused, when they can provide the clarifying and organizing ideas. Leadership ignites the circuit between the individual and the mass and thereby alters history.

It may alter history for better or for worse. Leaders have been responsible for the most extravagant follies and most monstrous crimes that have beset suffering humanity. They have also been vital in such gains as humanity has made in individual freedom, religious and racial tolerance, social justice and respect for human rights.

There is no sure way to tell in advance who is going to lead for good and who for evil. But a glance at the gallery of men and women in *World Leaders—Past and Present* suggests some useful tests.

One test is this: do leaders lead by force or by persuasion? By command or by consent? Through most of history leadership was exercised by the divine right of authority. The duty of followers was to defer and to obey. "Theirs not to reason why,/ Theirs but to do and die." On occasion, as with the so-called "enlightened despots" of the 18th century in Europe, absolutist leadership was animated by humane purposes. More often, absolutism nourished the passion for domination, land, gold and conquest and resulted in tyranny.

The great revolution of modern times has been the revolution of equality. The idea that all people should be equal in their legal condition has undermined the old structure of authority, hierarchy and deference. The revolution of equality has had two contrary effects on the nature of leadership. For equality, as Alexis de Tocqueville pointed out in his great study *Democracy in America*, might mean equality in servitude as well as equality in freedom.

"I know of only two methods of establishing equality in the political world," Tocqueville wrote. "Rights must be given to every citizen, or none at all to anyone . . . save one, who is the master of all." There was no middle ground "between the sovereignty of all and the absolute power of one man." In his astonishing prediction of 20th-century totalitarian dictatorship, Tocqueville explained how the revolution of equality could lead to the *"Führerprinzip"* and more terrible absolutism than the world had ever known.

But when rights are given to every citizen and the sovereignty of all is established, the problem of leadership takes a new form, becomes more exacting than ever before. It is easy to issue commands and enforce them by the rope and the stake, the concentration camp and the *gulag.* It is much harder to use argument and achievement to overcome opposition and win consent. The Founding Fathers of the United States understood the difficulty. They believed that history had given them the opportunity to decide, as Alexander Hamilton wrote in the first Federalist Paper, whether men are indeed capable of basing government on "reflection and choice, or whether they are forever destined to depend . . . on accident and force."

Government by reflection and choice called for a new style of leadership and a new quality of followership. It required leaders to be responsive to popular concerns, and it required followers to be active and informed participants in the process. Democracy does not eliminate emotion from politics; sometimes it fosters demagoguery; but it is confident that, as the greatest of democratic leaders put it, you cannot fool all of the people all of the time. It measures leadership by results and retires those who overreach or falter or fail.

It is true that in the long run despots are measured by results too. But they can postpone the day of judgment, sometimes indefinitely, and in the meantime they can do infinite harm. It is also true that democracy is no guarantee of virtue and intelligence in government, for the voice of the people is not necessarily the voice of God. But democracy, by assuring the right of opposition, offers built-in resistance to the evils inherent in absolutism. As the theologian Reinhold Niebuhr summed it up, "Man's capacity for justice makes democracy possible, but man's inclination to injustice makes democracy necessary."

A second test for leadership is the end for which power is sought. When leaders have as their goal the supremacy of a master race or the promotion of totalitarian revolution or the acquisition and exploitation of colonies or the protection of greed and privilege or the preservation of personal power, it is likely that their leadership will do little to advance the cause of humanity. When their goal is the abolition of slavery, the liberation of women, the enlargement of opportunity for the poor and powerless, the extension of equal rights to racial minorities, the defense of the freedoms of expression and opposition, it is likely that their leadership will increase the sum of human liberty and welfare.

Leaders have done great harm to the world. They have also conferred great benefits. You will find both sorts in this series. Even "good" leaders must be regarded with a certain wariness. Leaders are not demigods; they put on their trousers one leg after another just like ordinary mortals. No leader is infallible, and every leader needs to be reminded of this at regular intervals. Irreverence irritates leaders but is their salvation. Unquestioning submission corrupts leaders and demands followers. Making a cult of a leader is always a mistake. Fortunately hero worship generates its own antidote. "Every hero," said Emerson, "becomes a bore at last."

The signal benefit the great leaders confer is to embolden the rest of us to live according to our own best selves, to be active, insistent, and resolute in affirming our own sense of things. For great leaders attest to the reality of human freedom against the supposed inevitabilities of history. And they attest to the wisdom and power that may lie within the most unlikely of us, which is why Abraham Lincoln remains the supreme example of great leadership. A great leader, said Emerson, exhibits new possibilities to all humanity. "We feed on genius. . . . Great men exist that there may be greater men."

Great leaders, in short, justify themselves by emancipating and empowering their followers. So humanity struggles to master its destiny, remembering with Alexis de Tocqueville: "It is true that around every man a fatal circle is traced beyond which he cannot pass; but within the wide verge of that circle he is powerful and free; as it is with man, so with communities."

1

"It's Worth a Look!"

An ingenious and fatal machine casts its long shadow over the pages of this story. It has a tall, strong wooden frame that is grooved along the inside edges to permit the raising and lowering of a heavy blade. The blade is raised by a system of lead weights and pulleys, and is designed to come down quickly, hurled to the base of the frame by its own weight. A movable wooden plank, large enough to lie on, is fitted into the frame close to the base, where two semicircular pieces of wood (the lunette) can open and shut to admit a medium-sized object and hold it in place in the path of the blade. It is a machine for cutting off heads.

In the years following the French Revolution, men and women scheduled for execution would be brought through the crowded streets of what was — or had been — perhaps the most beautiful and civilized city in the world: Paris, the capital of the great nation of France. The citizens of Paris would turn out in large numbers for the passing of these doomed prisoners. This huge, noisy crowd might be hostile and jeering, or sympathetic and tearful, or some unpredictable, potentially dangerous mixture of both. The condemned passed by in tall red carts, or tumbrels, drawn by horses. Each cart held

The public is a ferocious beast; one must either chain it up or flee from it.
—VOLTAIRE
18th-century
French philosopher

Danton was perhaps the Revolution's greatest public speaker. Whether agitating in a Paris café or speaking before government officials, Danton could sway the most stubborn of minds.

Portrait of King Louis XVI. The king's indecisiveness and inability to manage national resources eventually led to his downfall and the French Revolution.

five or six people. The prisoners' hair was chopped off short in back, and their clothing was loosened to expose their necks. Although it was difficult for the doomed to maintain their balance in the moving carts with their hands tied behind their backs, some stood and bravely faced the mob as it screamed insults, or sang patriotic songs, or threw rotten fruits and vegetables at the carts.

The deadly machine was set up on a high platform in a public square. The executioner had the condemned ride backwards, so that they would not see the contraption as they approached. But they could see all the excited people watching them, crowding into the square, hanging off ladders and lampposts, leaning out of windows. They could also see the big red cart waiting to carry their bodies to the graveyard.

One by one, their names were called. One by one, they were helped up the ladder to the scaffold, their hands still tied behind their backs. One by one, they were laid on the plank and the snug-fitting lunette closed around their necks. One by one (but one fewer each time), they could hear the blade come down, and the gasps and cheers of the crowd. One by one, they felt that deep, swift bite. . . .

The machine that brought death and justice so swiftly was considered both democratic and merciful. Although machines for cutting off heads had been used occasionally since the Middle Ages, the technology of decapitation was refined after the French Revolution, and the "guillotine," as the French called the new machine, is forever associated with that time. Before 1792, only aristocrats had the privilege of choosing to be beheaded if they were sentenced to death. Commoners found guilty of capital offenses were usually hanged, burned, or executed by other means that were considerably more painful than decapitation.

After the French Revolution, the newly-elected assembly decreed that since all men were equal under the law, all should be entitled to the same means of execution, which should be as swift and painless as possible. The deputy who first made this proposal was an eminent Parisian doctor, Joseph Ignace Guillotin, and he was assigned the task of finding the most humane method of carrying out the death sentence. Dr. Guillotin did not actually design the guillotine. In fact, he claimed that he had never seen the deadly machine in action. But for the rest of his life, people often stopped him in the street, laughed, and made chopping gestures with their hands.

> *At last I perceive that in revolutions the supreme power rests with the most abandoned.*
> —GEORGES JACQUES DANTON

Dr. Joseph Guillotin believed swift, painless execution should be the right of every condemned person. Despite Guillotin's democratic intentions, the excesses of the Revolution turned the instrument that bore his name into a symbol of evil.

Dr. Guillotin may have been squeamish, but the machine that bears his name was not. In the heyday of its activity, during the 502 days of the period of the Revolution known as the "Reign of Terror," more than 2,300 people were guillotined. The first elected representatives in the history of France had found it necessary to have some heads cut off, to establish the new freedoms they were claiming for all Frenchmen, and to protect the new republic they were creating. The Republic had enemies who would stop at nothing to destroy the new order and restore the privileges they had enjoyed under the old one.

But once the guillotine began its work, it was almost impossible to stop. Every turn of political fortune that brought new men to power also brought more executions. Each time those new leaders thought the Revolution and the bloodshed were finally over. But others, struggling for power or principles of their own, disagreed. So churchgoer turned against priest, neighbor against neighbor, friend against friend; and the guillotine kept busy.

On April 5, 1794, at the height of the Reign of Terror, three tumbrels rolled slowly along the familiar route from the Conciergerie prison to the scaffold at the Place de la Révolution (now the Place de la Concorde). The crowds were larger than usual: it was a beautiful day, and the men in the carts were very well known. One, a fiery journalist, sat and wept, talking brokenly about his beautiful wife and new baby. Another, an aristocrat who not five years before had stormed the great royal prison-fortress of the Bastille during the first battle of the Revolution, sneered coldly at the mob he once had led.

The man who drew the eyes of the mob was taller and bigger and stronger than the others. He was a man of tremendous energy, a statesman who had protected the fragile French Republic in its greatest peril, an orator who had stirred his fellow citizens to action with his impassioned speeches. Georges Jacques Danton had been the most popular and powerful man in the city not so many months ago. In his courage and vitality he seemed to symbolize the heroic city itself, and one could hardly think of

the Revolution without thinking of him. Surely the people would not, could not, let him die.

Yet some in the crowd feared his ambition, or had grudges of their own against him — a man who makes bold decisions makes many enemies. These individuals waited eagerly for the death sentence to be carried out. Others, no doubt, remembered him with affection and loyalty, and hoped for a rescue. The majority, however, was simply curious to see whether this hero's death would be worthy of his life.

As his doomed companions in the tumbrel wept or prayed or cursed, Danton prepared to die. He stood in the cart and laughed and joked, comforting his friends and calling out to the crowd. In order to give the other condemned men the courage to die bravely, Danton was the last to mount the scaffold. His final words echo down the corridors of history with the style and spirit of this most complicated and unusual man. "Show my head to the people," he said to the executioner, "it's worth a look!"

The guillotine was a very public and efficient means of execution. When it was first used in Paris, disappointed spectators said it was *too* good at its job; the execution was so quick that onlookers complained that they could not actually see it.

17

2

The Republican

Georges Jacques Danton was born on October 26, 1759, in a sleepy town in the northeast of France called Arcis-sur-Aube. This town of fewer than 3,000 inhabitants had for centuries undergone very little change. Loyal subjects of the faraway king lived here beside the meandering Aube River and occupied themselves, just as their ancestors had, with local matters: the weather, the crops that could be grown in the region's poor, chalky soil (mostly rye and buckwheat), the local church, neighborhood gossip, and family matters. The idea of "France" — a great nation to which the residents of Arcis owed some larger allegiance — rarely troubled their minds. In times of drought or famine, perhaps, they might look to the king for help. More frequently, however, the king would look to them — for taxes to support his elaborate court, or soldiers to fight his wars.

At the time of Danton's birth, France had a population of around 25 million, and most of the people lived on farms or in the little towns and villages of the countryside. This tranquil world was about to be roughly awakened from its long medieval slumber, its inhabitants transformed from passive subjects of a king into citizens with a say in their government. Soon France's king would be dethroned and decapitated, its simple home-loving

Twenty times he courted death, twenty times he escaped.
—HENRI BÉRAUD
French historian, on
Danton's youth

Portrait of Danton. As a boy Danton showed the spirit and adventurous nature that would eventually make him one of France's most influential leaders.

Queen Marie-Antoinette married into France's royal family when she was 14. A strong-willed and sophisticated woman, she never won the hearts of her subjects but rather went to her grave with haughty dignity.

countrymen changed into fierce, patriotic soldiers and citizens, carrying a new idea, with a new sort of energy, across the map of Europe. Danton, the fifth child (and first son) of a lawyer active in local affairs, would play a large part in the violent awakening of small towns such as Arcis, and in the extraordinary transformation, for both good and bad, of France itself.

One might almost have guessed at this child's future by his powerful physical presence and irrepressible boldness. In an age that considered swimming an exotic and dangerous practice, young Georges spent many happy hours splashing in the Aube River. The boy survived an early bout with pneumonia and another with smallpox, a disease that left his face pitted with scars. In addition, several unusual battles with farm animals had altered his appearance. According to one story, he used to sneak out to the fields to drink milk directly from the cows' udders until one day an angry bull split his lip with its horn. When he attempted to get even with the bull, his nose was broken in the tussle. Later on, a herd of pigs knocked him down and trampled him, leaving him scarred and seriously injured. Some people who knew him as an adult described him as ugly, with his scars and broken nose, but he seems to have had the courageous spirit and confidence that our age calls charisma. For all his ugliness, he was a passionate admirer of women, and they frequently returned his affections.

Danton's father died before his son reached his third birthday, and Danton's mother and uncle were left to supervise the unruly boy's upbringing. Since Danton did poorly in all the subjects he studied in school except Latin, he was sent to a seminary in the nearby town of Troyes to study for the Catholic priesthood. He continued to display a remarkable facility for languages at the seminary, adding English and Italian to his Latin. Yet he still had no aptitude for most of his schoolwork and no desire to be a priest. He claimed that he found the religious atmosphere of the seminary stifling. When he was allowed to move to a private room in town, he soon mastered all his subjects.

One incident from these early days provides a good picture of the boy he was, and more than a hint of the man he would become. In those days, teachers punished students by striking them sharply on the fingers with a ruler. Danton's friend Paré could not recite his assigned text one morning, but he refused to put out his hands for punishment.

> *Independent, fearless, quarrelsome, he ran about the country, swam in the river, fought those who wanted to fight, as well as those who didn't.*
> —HENRI BÉRAUD
> French historian, on
> Danton's youth

The priest who was teaching the class was furious, but Danton rose to speak in Paré's defense. The youthful Danton already possessed the qualities that would make him one of the most powerful men in France: passion, wit, intelligence, and a powerful, booming voice. He spoke so persuasively against corporal punishment that the head of the school decided to outlaw the practice, and both the student and the teacher involved in this incident remained Danton's lifelong friends.

He must at some point have changed his mind about physical punishment. Otherwise Danton, with his ability to shape public opinion, might have been able to prevent the guillotine from darkening the Revolution with its long shadow, and he himself might have lived to play with his grandchildren.

Reims Cathedral was the traditional coronation place for the French monarchy. Legend has it that the 16-year-old Danton ran away from school and sneaked into the cathedral to witness the crowning of the king he would later help to force from the throne.

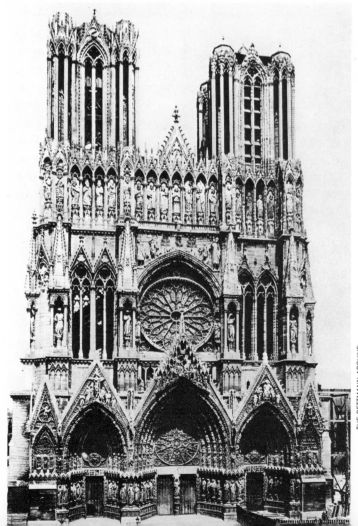

Another story about Danton's youth is even more ironic. On June 11, 1775, a great ceremony took place 70 miles from Troyes in the cathedral at Reims, the traditional site of French coronations. The large, gawky, pleasant-faced dauphin (the name for the eldest son of a French king), accompanied by Marie-Antoinette, his beautiful young Austrian wife, was crowned King Louis XVI of France. One of Danton's teachers made the coronation the subject of an essay assignment. Danton did not come to class on the day the essay was due. Instead, he managed to travel to Reims — no easy feat for a 16-year-old boy in those days — where he talked his way into the cathedral and witnessed the event for himself. The boy who would one day help to topple the king heard Louis XVI swear "to rule according to the law and welfare of the nation." Unfortunately, Danton's essay — late, but undoubtedly written with a certain flair—has not survived.

George Washington and the marquis de Lafayette. At age 19 Lafayette defied King Louis XVI by joining the American war for independence. The French would soon follow America's example and found their own republic.

The impetuous boldness of his trip to see the king's coronation, and his passionate defense of his poor friend against the absolute authority of the priest, helped earn Danton his schoolboy nickname, "the Republican" (one who believes that the power of the government should be in the hands of the people and their elected representatives).

Danton "the Republican" was a product of his age. New ideas were in the air. In 1776, the American colonists began a war to win independence from their distant king, Great Britain's George III. The revolutionaries adopted Thomas Jefferson's Declaration of Independence, which stated "that all men are created equal, that they are endowed by their Creator with certain unalienable Rights, that among these are Life, Liberty and the pursuit of Happiness." After the colonists won the war they created a republic, the United States of America, in which all citizens had a voice. Danton and his friends had not yet read Jefferson's declaration, but revolutionary ideas were spreading and many of them had been French to begin with.

The American Revolutionary War won the colonists independence from Great Britain's King George III. The new country's rejection of a monarchy inspired a wave of antiroyalist sentiment throughout Europe.

Voltaire, one of 18th-century France's most distinguished philosophers, was imprisoned in the Bastille for libel as a young man. His preference for reason above religion challenged the monarchy, since kings claimed to rule by divine right.

Jefferson and his American colleagues were the natural heirs of an extraordinary group of French philosophers such as Voltaire and Jean-Jacques Rousseau who began to scrutinize the sleepy world in which their contemporaries lived. They questioned the blind acceptance many held for the larger institutions that shaped their lives, such as the Church and the monarchy. These philosophers, who prided themselves on thinking that was unclouded by prejudice and superstition, examined the old world in a bright new light — the light of reason. In fact, the era in which they lived came to be known as "The Age of Reason." As Danton grew into manhood the legacy of these men, and the American revolutionaries who applied their ideas, began to take hold in France.

When he finished his studies in 1780, Danton decided to seek his fortune in the wider world. Arcis-sur-Aube did not offer sufficient scope for his talents and ambitions, so he bid his relatives a solemn farewell and hitched a ride on a public coach driven by a friend of the family. He was 21 years old, with very little cash but great expectations, and off to seek his fortune in Paris.

With children use force, with men reason; such is the natural order of things. The wise man requires no law.
—JEAN-JACQUES ROUSSEAU
18th-century philosopher

Engraved by W.H. Mote.

DANTON.

3

Monsieur d'Anton

Danton's uncle had given him a letter of rec-
ommendation to a Parisian lawyer named Vinot,
and Danton became Vinot's clerk shortly after his
arrival in Paris. He worked hard for Vinot, and he
learned not only the complicated business of the
various Paris courts, but also the streets and
rhythms and mysteries of the great city itself. In his
spare time Danton studied hard, hoping to become
a lawyer himself. He read many of the great thinkers
and writers, including Voltaire, Rousseau, John
Milton, Dante, and William Shakespeare. In spite of
his labors, Danton still managed to find time for his
eccentric hobby, swimming. His exercises in the
Seine River usually drew a crowd.

In those days, it was possible to acquire degrees
at certain universities with a minimum of effort, if
the right price was paid. Jean-Paul Marat, the fiery
journalist who was Danton's colleague in later years,
bought a medical degree in Scotland, from the University of Edinburgh. In October 1784, when Danton felt he had saved enough money and learned all
he could as a clerk, he purchased a law degree from
the University of Reims.

> *He drowned all difficulties,
> all rivalries and all hatreds in
> the torrent of action.*
> —JEAN-JOSEPH JAURÈS
> French Socialist politician,
> on Danton

**As a young man Danton was interested more in using
politics to advance his career than in changing France's
political and social systems. He even altered the spelling
of his name, pretending to be an aristocrat in order to
encourage business.**

Radical journalist Jean-Paul Marat was beloved by the lower classes of Paris. Like many of the Revolution's leaders, Marat frequently advocated violence. He once stated that 200,000 heads would have to roll in order to maintain public order.

Law was not the only thing on the young man's mind, however. A short walk from the Paris law courts was the Café de l'École, a congenial establishment run by a man named Charpentier who was also a wealthy tax collector. (Men paid to become tax collectors in those days, then kept a share of all the taxes they took in.) Danton had dinner most nights at the Café de l'École, where he enjoyed a simple meal, an occasional game of dominoes, and the conversation of Charpentier and the young lawyers who gathered there. Danton also enjoyed chatting with Charpentier's Italian wife — in her own language — and with Gabrielle, their lovely young daughter. It was soon clear that Danton cared for Gabrielle, and equally clear that she returned his feelings. But he was hardly in a position to take a wife.

His position was about to change. In the Paris legal profession of the time it took money to make money. All important jobs, like Charpentier's tax collecting, were for sale, but Danton's practice was small and most of his clients were poor, leaving him with no capital to invest in a high position. Nevertheless, an opportunity soon presented itself. An acquaintance of Danton's, Huet de Paisy, was preparing to resign his prestigious post as counsel to the king's bench, and he hoped to sell the office to Danton.

The matter is worth a close look, because the mysterious nature of Danton's finances raises large questions about the motives and actions of his later life. Huet had bought his counsel's office thirteen years before for 30,000 livres. Danton now agreed to buy it for 78,000 livres, a huge sum that he assembled by borrowing heavily from family, friends, and professional moneylenders. When Danton learned that Huet still owed money to the heirs of the man from whom he had bought the office in the first place, he agreed to make payments on this debt as well.

Danton had assumed a crushing financial burden, especially since he planned to marry and begin raising a family. It seemed unlikely that the fees to be gained from this new position would ever be sufficient to pay all the bills. Nevertheless, Danton agreed to buy Huet's post, and shortly thereafter, on June 14, 1787, he married Gabrielle. He was 27, she 24, and perhaps the future looked rosier to them than it had any right to.

May 5, 1789, was the opening day of the Estates General, a meeting of elected representatives from all over France. King Louis XVI convened the assembly to address the nation's growing financial crisis, but many of the deputies insisted that the group consider other, more popular grievances.

Angered by the independence of the National Assembly, Louis tried to stop the deputies from meeting by barring them from the palace at Versailles. The defiant representatives of the Third Estate sought a new location for their meetings and eventually continued their debates on the royal tennis courts.

The bridegroom sailed through the difficult examination required before he could argue cases before the king. He improvised a striking speech — in Latin — on "the moral and political situation of our country as it affects the administration of justice." He dealt with the potentially dangerous topic by eloquently counseling moderation and sacrifice. "Woe to those who provoke revolutions, woe to those who make them!" he declared. He was admitted as counsel to the king's bench.

As he embarked on this prestigious new career, Danton began to sign his name "d'Anton." A "de" or "d' " before the last name implies that the person who bears the name is an aristocrat. The little word means "of," as in the "duc de Richelieu" (the duke of Richelieu) or the "comte d'Alembert" (the count of Alembert). Altering one's name in this fashion was an old trick. The English novelist Daniel Foe, author of *Robinson Crusoe*, is remembered today under the more impressive-sounding name he adopted, Daniel Defoe. Perhaps "d'Anton" felt that a loftier name would help him in his career, especially as he would now be arguing cases before the king himself. For a time, anyway, he became "Georges Jacques of Anton," a harmless yet surprising affectation for a man who was called "the Republican" in his school days and who was to become a famous revolutionary in his maturity.

As "d'Anton" and his new bride began their life together, France was perched on the brink of sweeping change, change that would be swift, comprehensive, and bloody. Danton was a natural leader, and he had a gift for stirring, delighting, and persuading people with his dramatic oratory. He soon found himself — and worked hard to keep himself — in the thick of things.

The first real step in the French Revolution was taken by the king himself. An inefficient economy and long, costly wars had devastated the government treasury. Desperately needing money, King

A decree of the National Assembly, printed between pillars that read "Live free or die" and "Nation, law, king." Although the assembly still accepted monarchy at the time, it is significant that "king" is mentioned *after* "nation" and "law."

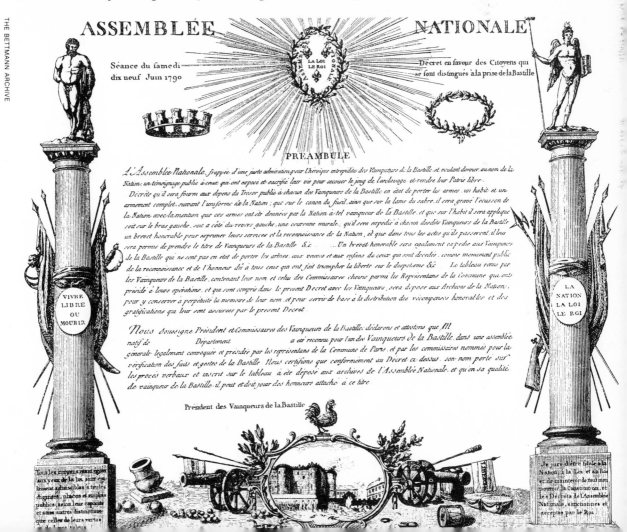

While the representatives to the Constituent Assembly made history at Versailles, the people of Paris began making history in the streets. Mobilized by powerful speakers such as Danton, Parisians began taking up arms in 1789.

Louis XVI hoped that the common people would help him squeeze it out of the nobility while the nobility would help him squeeze some more out of the common people. He also hoped that both groups would help him squeeze more money out of the clergy (the religious community: priests, monks, bishops, etc.). The king summoned the Estates General, an assembly of representatives from those three different groups — known as estates — from all over his kingdom. (The First Estate was the clergy, the Second Estate the nobility, and the Third Estate, which was larger than the other two estates combined, included basically everybody else.) When the representatives arrived at the king's court at Versailles on May 5, 1789, to help Louis XVI prevent a national bankruptcy, many were shocked at the luxury and extravagance they found there.

These busy deputies had not left their homes and jobs and come all the way to Versailles only to rubber-stamp the king's latest financial scheme. The representatives had worked hard in their home districts to assemble *cahiers de doléances*, notebooks detailing local complaints to be brought to the attention of the king that were vigorously debated and patiently compiled all over France. This Estates General, for better or worse, had a mind of its own.

No French king had summoned an assembly of national representatives since the Parliament of 1614, and no one really knew how the Estates General should function — how its members should be chosen, what procedures it should follow, what power it should have, and how that power should be divided between the representatives of the three different estates. All was improvisation and history in the making. Seemingly unimportant actions — a bold speech by an unknown middle-class deputy, a generous response from an influential clergyman, a selfish act from a privileged nobleman, or a moment of weakness from the bewildered king — could have enormous consequences. Fundamental questions of the economic and political life of the nation churned beneath the surface, but the personalities of the participants did much to shape the events.

The members of the Third Estate outnumbered the other representatives, and dissension prevented the privileged estates from voting in a bloc anyway. There were many poor country priests in France who shared the lives and grievances of their parishioners and resented the easy lives of the rich monks and bishops. These priests voted with the Third Estate. There were also many aristocrats who lived simple lives in the provinces, whose ties were with the country towns and villages, not with the ultra-fashionable and haughty courtiers of Versailles who made up the Second Estate.

Many representatives refused to act on the king's urgent financial proposals until they got their own way about the agenda for the Estates General and were assured that certain public grievances would be redressed. They had time on their side, and the king, with his nearly bankrupt government, did not. He began to give in to their wishes. As more sympathetic members of the privileged classes joined the deputies of the Third Estate, this surprising Estates General gave itself a proud new name: the National Assembly.

The young revolutionary Camille Desmoulins incites a crowd to arms at the Palais Royal. The discontented working people of Paris and their leaders were much more radical — and dangerous — than the assembly.

A woman watches anxiously as armed crowds march through the streets of Paris. Both citizens and officials lived in fear of the violence unleashed by the Revolution. The words "Long live liberty" have been painted on her shutters.

CULVER PICTURES

King Louis XVI reacted angrily and ordered their meeting place "closed for repairs," but the persistant representatives of the Third Estate met at the nearby royal tennis court and swore a solemn oath never to abandon their work until they had achieved the goals they had set for themselves: "to settle the constitution of the realm, to bring about the regeneration of public order, and to uphold the true principles of the monarchy."

Although they were defying the king, the representatives still believed in and intended to serve their sovereign. Louis, for his part, found little consolation in their professions of loyalty. He tried to adjourn the assembly, but his commands went unheeded. "We shall not budge from our places here," said the comte de Mirabeau, a liberal nobleman representing the city of Aix who supported the Third Estate, "except at the point of the bayonet." The astronomer Jean-Sylvain Bailly, representing the Third Estate of Paris and elected as the first president of the assembly, went even further. "I take it," he said, "that no one can give orders to the assembled nation." The intimidated king ordered the clergy and nobles to unite with the Third Estate in order to avoid violence. The new group adopted the name of "Constituent Assembly" on July 9, 1789.

The members of the assembly were not the only ones interested in gaining power from the weakened monarch. An almost continual excitement, a surging of emotions — from fear to rage to joy — could be felt in the streets of the capital. The population of Paris was over 500,000 — five times that of any other city in France. It had elected its share of deputies to the assembly, but there were many people in Paris eager to be directly involved in the shaping of events, and other leaders were naturally thrust forward.

Men made impromptu speeches in the streets or stood on tables in the gardens of the Palais Royal, a famous public meeting place, and attempted to direct the energies of the explosive Parisians. These were not the same sort of individuals — polite, scholarly, professional men, for the most part — who had gone off to debate before the king at Versailles. Paris had more than its share of poor men — one out of five Parisians needed public relief — and poor men were not allowed to vote for deputies. The interests of the poor were not represented in the assembly nearly as effectively or dramatically as the poor could represent themselves, when they followed their own chosen leaders and turned themselves into a passionate, dangerous mob.

An uncomfortable truth became increasingly clear to the members of the Constituent Assembly, who would soon swear to help restore "the public order." The wheel of revolution, now turning away from the king, had not come to a full stop. Some of the political power expressed in the election of the representatives to the assembly, and then by the deputies' stubborn courage in defying the king, overflowed where those in power least wanted it to go — into the narrow streets and alleys of Paris. Georges Jacques Danton, his aristocratic "d' " gone for good, was just the sort of man to be there in the Palais Royal, standing on a table and stirring up the mob.

> The systems that fail are those that rely on the permanency of human nature, and not on its growth and development. The error of Louis XVI was that he thought human nature would always be the same. The result of his error was the French Revolution.
> —OSCAR WILDE
> 19th-century British writer

4

The King of the Cordeliers

We don't know much about what Danton was doing and thinking in the years leading up to the Revolution. He and Gabrielle had had a son in 1788, but the boy died a year later. The young lawyer had worked hard to build up his law practice and pay some of his debts.

Danton did very good work for one of his early clients, Barentin, an influential public official, and through him became acquainted with the king's minister of finance, the aristocratic Archbishop Loménie de Brienne, who came from a small town near Arcis. Danton submitted a detailed and ambitious program to the minister, recommending certain reforms — primarily concessions to the poor from the nobility and the clergy — that would make it much easier for the king to lead his increasingly rebellious subjects. Unfortunately, the conservative archbishop was unconvinced; but his friend Barentin was impressed. When Barentin became minister of justice he asked Danton to join the government as secretary of the chancellery. But Danton thought it was too late for the king and his government to take the lead in shaping France's political life; too much time had already been lost. He turned down Barentin's offer. Events — and Danton with them — would take a rougher course.

His words were not only words — they were France's energy made concrete, a cry from the nation's heart.
—JULES MICHELET
19th-century French historian, on Danton's speeches

If the Revolution had not taken place, Danton's charm and professional skill would probably have secured him a prestigious government job. Instead, his combination of vision and opportunism made him an ideal revolutionary leader.

The meeting place of the Cordelier Club has since become a museum. Many of the workingmen who met here to listen to speeches and discuss politics eventually joined in the revolutionary frenzy of the violent street crowds.

As Paris became a center for political dissent, many citizens began to fear that the king would punish the residents of the capital. On July 13, 1789, Danton made a dramatic speech before a group of men who met to discuss the important questions of the day in an abandoned monastery in Danton's neighborhood, the Cordeliers district. His words give some flavor of the fear, excitement, and disorder of those hectic days. Danton warned that "an army of 30,000 soldiers stood ready to descend on Paris, loot the city, and massacre its inhabitants." His powerful voice rose to a crescendo as he urged his listeners to take up arms. The people of the Cordeliers district, roused by his speech, formed their own army, and Danton volunteered to join it.

While Danton stirred up the Cordeliers, his good friend Camille Desmoulins, a fearless republican journalist who stammered when he was not addressing a crowd, made a similar speech at the Palais Royal. Thousands of Parisians were stirred to action by these two men and other popular leaders.

After a day of rumors and skirmishes, the Paris mob, searching for guns and ammunition, attacked the towering prison-fortress of the Bastille, one of the most hated symbols of royal authority and oppression in the world. In the battle, which lasted more than two hours, 98 citizens were killed; but the mob had its revenge. After the governor of the prison, the marquis de Launay, surrendered, he was murdered by the mob. The victorious citizens, delirious with triumph, surged through the streets of the city with his bloody head on a pike. The day of the riot, July 14, 1789, is celebrated as Bastille Day, France's Independence Day.

Somehow, both Danton and Desmoulins missed the combat. Danton, however, was heard from early the next morning. After "inspecting" the Bastille with a few of his comrades from the Cordeliers battalion, he managed to "capture" the man who had been put in charge of the prison after its surrender. It was a comic episode — Danton identifying himself as "Captain" Danton, his disorderly little band dragging the poor man around Paris until he was finally identified as a political ally and freed — but it could have had tragic consequences. "Captain" Danton and his men nearly had to fight the mob to keep their prisoner from being murdered.

The boldness and authority Danton demonstrated in this near disaster bolstered his reputation as a leader. Sixty Paris districts had been formed in April 1789 to choose the men who would then vote for the deputies to the Estates General. After their electoral duties were fulfilled, however, these electors refused to go out of business. Instead, they began to function as 60 independent units, with their own small legislatures and their own heads of government. After his "military" adventure, "Captain" Danton was swept into office as president of his increasingly powerful district. It soon became apparent that Paris, France's largest and most politically active city, ruled the nation, and the districts ruled Paris.

Cannon being brought through the streets of Paris to Montmartre. Military officers knew that many of their soldiers would refuse to fire on the citizens, since they were sympathetic to the Revolution's aims. The lawlessness would worsen along with the national economy.

One of the primary causes behind the storming of the Bastille was the king's dismissal of Jacques Necker, the popular minister of finance who had persuaded the king to call the Estates General in the first place. After the fall of the Bastille, the king recalled Necker and appeared before the assembly to calm things down, but the trouble was in Paris, not Versailles. The king knew he had to muster support from the unruly mobs of the capital. Taking his life in his hands, he went to Paris on July 17. The citizens cheered him for his bravery, but the violence had not yet ended. On July 23 the mob captured the man who had temporarily replaced Necker, hanged him (and for good measure, his son-in-law as well) and again paraded the severed heads on bloody pikes.

Meanwhile, in Versailles, the assembly went about its business. On August 4, 1789, the deputies voted to abolish all the remaining ties and obligations of feudalism, the complex system of social and economic organization that had existed since the Middle Ages. Most of the people of France applauded this move, although many members of the privileged estates regretted the end of a system that gave the Church and nobility so many rights and benefits at the expense of the rest of the people. Throughout August the assembly debated the Declaration of the Rights of Man, which would become the prologue to the Constitution of 1791. This historic declaration, based on the American Declaration of Independence, stated that every citizen had the right to liberty, equality, property, and security.

King Louis delayed his public acceptance of the assembly's decrees and secretly summoned Flemish troops to Versailles. Since so many French soldiers sympathized with the people, these mercenaries (hired soldiers) were the only troops he could count on. The arrival of the foreign mercenaries caused great fury in Paris. Danton wrote a manifesto denouncing the king's actions that was posted all over Paris.

The city was both angry and afraid. The economic problems that had caused the king to call the Estates General in the first place had only grown

worse. Many wealthy employers had fled the country after the fall of the Bastille, and their former workers and servants swelled the ranks of the unemployed. The people of France also faced a great shortage of bread, the staple of the national diet.

The ugly mood in Paris led to one of the most startling and unlikely scenes of the Revolution. On October 5, 1789, a crowd of women demanding bread seized arms from the town hall and set off for Versailles. Danton, whose manifesto had helped fuel the march, had second thoughts and kept the Cordeliers volunteers from accompanying this ragtag army. But the soldiers of other district militias insisted on following these angry, hungry women, who were, after all, their own mothers, sisters, and wives.

A dramatic engraving depicting the people of Paris carrying the commander of the prison garrison from the Bastille. In the popular imagination the dungeons of the Bastille were a potent symbol of repression. After his capture the commander's severed head was paraded through the streets on a pike.

The commander of these troops was the marquis
de Lafayette, the daring, young aristocrat who had
already demonstrated his deep devotion to the cause
of liberty by serving in the American Revolutionary
War under General George Washington. He had also
played a large role in drafting the Declaration of the
Rights of Man. Lafayette passionately believed that
liberty should be guaranteed by a constitution and
a legislature, such as the Constituent Assembly, but

The king arrives at the Hôtel de Ville (the town hall). Only days after the Bastille was captured, Louis XVI traveled to Paris and donned a tricolor ribbon, a symbol of the Revolution. Though his bravery was recognized, it did not prevent further riots.

that the king should continue to lead the French government.

Although Lafayette thought that the "Bread March of the Women" would do no good, his soldiers forced the issue. If he did not lead them, they would go without him. Sending word to the king that he was coming (and begging him not to order his guards to fire on the mob), Lafayette led his volunteers to Versailles.

Peasants burn papers that gave the aristocracy virtual control over their lives. In order to restore order after the Bastille attack the Constituent Assembly's noblemen voluntarily abolished their rights over the people, against the will of the king.

The women got there several hours before the soldiers and went straight to the assembly. The surprised representatives were only too happy to make use of this display of popular feeling. They added their own demand — that the king stop stalling and accept their decrees — to the women's cries for bread and the dismissal of the Flemish troops. The astonished king met with some of the protesters, then avoided making a decision for several hours. Realizing that his refusal would lead to violence, Louis finally agreed to accept "without qualification" the protesters' demands. The king approved the abolition of feudalism, the Declaration of the Rights of Man, and all the articles of the constitution so far decreed by the assembly.

But Louis's surrender came too late and too grudgingly to appease his discontented subjects. The triumphant mob, now supported by the tardy guardsmen, made one further demand: that the king and his family leave the luxurious palace at Versailles and come back to Paris, where they would be closer to the people (and the people could keep a closer watch on them). Again, Louis XVI had no real choice. Trusting his safety to the personal guarantees of Lafayette, he agreed to let himself and his family be taken to the turbulent capital.

Despite the king's acceptance of their demands, some of the women in the mob broke into the palace and threatened Queen Marie-Antoinette. The queen was considered to be proud and cold, and her Austrian birth made her even more unpopular. She managed to save herself by fleeing to the king's chamber in her nightgown, just ahead of the menacing intruders.

The next day, the victorious women and soldiers of Paris returned home and took the king of France with them. With Louis gone, the Constituent Assembly had little reason to stay at Versailles. The assembly decided to follow the king to Paris, although more than 300 of its upper-class members, fearing the Paris mob, resigned rather than face the Parisians. The mob, in capturing the king, had also captured the assembly, and, in fact, the Revolution itself.

The scene of the drama had changed. The king and his family settled into the relatively cramped quarters of Paris's Tuileries Palace. The Constituent Assembly began meeting nearby. The wheel of revolution had turned again, and the power of the Paris leaders had increased enormously.

But a large question remained. Could the men who stirred up the Paris mob really control it? Danton was widely hailed now for his part in inspiring the march on Versailles. Could he and his friends, or their rivals, really bring the wheel of revolution to a stop? Desmoulins thought so. "It is finished," he wrote in his journal, "the patriots have triumphed!" Time would tell.

Figures representing "Liberty" and "Equality." "Equality" is holding the Declaration of the Rights of Man, which proclaimed that "Men are born free and equal in rights."

5

Rivals and a Rising Star

The popular president of the Cordeliers district worked tirelessly to increase his power and influence as dissension continued to rock Paris. He even went to visit the beleaguered king in the Tuileries to "thank" him for coming to Paris. But Danton was not the only man in the city maneuvering to inherit some of the power the king had been forced to surrender. Danton's rivals included Bailly, the hero of the early days of the Estates General, who was now mayor of Paris, and Lafayette, who commanded the National Guard. Danton looked for ways to limit the power of these two men while increasing his own. An incident involving the radical journalist Jean-Paul Marat soon provided an excellent opportunity.

Marat was an outspoken advocate for the poor who specialized in vicious attacks on his political opponents. His venomous journal was called *The People's Friend*, and that title extended to the man himself as his popularity grew. When he decided that Bailly was not serving the people's interests, he published a savage attack on the mayor. In response, Bailly ordered Lafayette to arrest Marat.

He rendered an immense service to the Revolution and to his country by crushing with his strong words all thoughts of weakness and by inciting everyone to hope and to action.
—JEAN-JOSEPH JAURÈS
French Socialist politician,
on Danton

In the early years of the Revolution Danton prospered financially and broadened his political power base. He managed to hold his own among powerful rivals by manipulating political circumstances to his own advantage.

Maximilien Robespierre won widespread support in the nation's capital as president of the Jacobin Club. Like Danton, he was a lawyer, but there the similarity ended. Robespierre was driven by idealism, while Danton tempered his revolutionary fervor with pragmatism and self-interest.

Danton, as president of one of Paris's 60 districts, was nominally under the authority of the mayor, but the Cordeliers district was so powerful and politically active that he could operate with considerable independence. Marat knew this, so he called for Danton and the Cordeliers to save him. Whatever he personally thought of Marat, Danton was glad to have a public battle to fight with Bailly and Lafayette. He came to Marat's rescue, using his legal expertise to challenge the arrest warrant and even risking a battle between the Cordeliers militia and Lafayette's troops. The popular outcry in Paris soon forced Bailly and Lafayette to back down, and Danton won additional prestige as the protector of "the People's Friend." When an attempt was made to arrest Danton for his part in Marat's defense, the people took their protest straight to the assembly. Unsurprisingly, the deputies sided with the angry mob, and Danton's popularity continued to rise.

A stiff, priggish, middle-class lawyer from the city of Arras, Maximilien Robespierre, began to emerge as Danton's most important rival for the hearts and minds of the Parisians. Robespierre was the president of the radical Jacobin Club, which took its name from the monastery in which it held its meetings. (Revolutionary French societies began to call themselves "clubs" at this time, because the English word also meant "weapon.") The Jacobins were enormously influential, with their own newsletter and local branches throughout the country. The men of the Jacobin Club were generally better educated, wealthier, and more powerful than Danton's Cordeliers.

When Danton was finally accepted for membership in the Jacobin Club, he got off to a bad start by delivering an emotional Cordelier-style speech. The Jacobins were much too refined and sophisticated for these old tricks. In time Danton learned how to make himself listened to in both places — with subtle orations for the Jacobins and impassioned harangues for the Cordeliers.

Danton and Robespierre were both brilliant and courageous revolutionary leaders, but their personalities were very different. Robespierre, known as "the Incorruptible" for his famed virtuousness and purity, was cold, hard, distant — a man of ideals and intellect. Danton was warm, easygoing, sociable — a man of passions and heart. For now, these natural rivals were uneasy allies in the Revolution.

Danton's imperfections, alleged or real, may have played an important part in shaping the policies — even the destiny — of his country. When he married Gabrielle, he was greatly in debt. By 1790, however,

> *Danton was not the kind of man to forget his own interests and his main concern may have been to provide himself and his friends with the means of gratifying their rather expensive tastes.*
> —NORMAN HAMPSON
> British historian

his life seemed to be increasingly comfortable, even luxurious, and his debts were being paid off with surprising speed. His visible income did not account for this prosperity. Various witnesses — often enemies of Danton — claimed that Danton was always well provided with an invisible income: bribes.

During the entire course of his public career, Danton is charged with accepting a dazzling assortment of bribes. Lafayette contended that he was in the pay of the king. Others believed that he took money from his friend (and the king's cousin), the popular, liberal duke of Orléans, Louis-Philippe. The duke represented Paris in the assembly, joined the Jacobin Club, and even changed his name to Philippe Égalité (égalité is the French word for "equality"). There was, for a time, much talk of the duke ruling the country as a regent for the king's young son, and Danton may have taken money to advance this project.

Other witnesses made even more serious charges, claiming that Danton accepted bribes from the enemies of France: the Spanish ambassador, the British prime minister, and the Austrian emperor. Some historians deduce — from the bits and pieces of available evidence, from the testimony of hostile witnesses, and from certain otherwise mysterious actions or omissions of Danton's — that he gladly accepted any money that was offered to him, from any source. There is no absolute proof, but the accumulation of circumstantial evidence is certainly persuasive.

The reality of this bribe taking may not be quite as bad as it sounds to the law-abiding citizens of a stable government. Robespierre was called "the Incorruptible" because his integrity was so unique. No one would ever have called Danton "the Incorruptible," and he probably would not have appreciated it if they had. These Frenchmen were, after all, making up new rules for everything as they went along; and money and privilege had always accompanied power.

Danton seems to have followed his own course, by his own lights, throughout his career; his mixture of courage, cunning, and independence in the area of foreign policy would soon bring the new nation safely through its most perilous hours. If, at the same time, he bent the law to pay his debts, which of his contemporaries, besides Robespierre, could criticize him? It is quite possible that Danton accepted bribes but did nothing to earn them, or that he accepted money to support positions he already believed in. At his trial in 1794, Danton responded to the bribery charges with a characteristic joke. Men like him could not be bought, he said; they were beyond price. Danton may have allowed himself to be frequently paid for, but never bought.

As the assembly worked to draw up the Constitution of 1791, Mirabeau maneuvered to keep the king at the helm of the government, the Paris rivals jockeyed for power, and the revolutionary cauldron continued to simmer. The Constituent Assembly, attempting to gain some control over the Paris mob, reorganized the districts, and Danton had a major setback. The Cordeliers district disappeared in the reorganization.

Like the Cordelier Club, the headquarters of the Jacobin Club was a former monastery, a location that was especially appropriate for the Jacobins, given the self-denying habits of their leader, Maximilien Robespierre.

ENGLISH CHANNEL

Lille •

Le Havre
Caen •
Evreux •
Versailles
Rouen
ILE-DE-FRANCE
• Reims
• Paris
• Arcis-sur-Aube
Seine

BRITTANY
NORMANDY

• Renne

• Nantes

VENDÉE

BURGUNDY

• Dijon

ALPS

BAY OF BISCAY

• Limoges
Lyon •

• Grenoble

Rhone

• Bourdeaux

Nimes •
PROVENCE

Toulouse •
• Marseille

PYRENEES

MEDITERRANEAN SEA

BARRY SIMON

Map of France. The Constituent Assembly tried to establish a program of reform for the whole country. Sweeping changes in the national and local governments and restrictions on the power and property of the Church were more controversial in the countryside than in Paris.

This setback may have been a blessing in disguise: Danton needed a larger pond in order to become a bigger fish. He ran for office in the city government and became a municipal councilor. Danton quickly rose through the ranks to become one of Paris's 16 administrators. His good fortune extended into his private life: in May 1790 Gabrielle had a second child, a boy.

During this period, the assembly stagnated in endless constitutional debates while the Tuileries Palace was a beehive of secret counterrevolutionary activity. Louis XVI now greatly regretted that he had come to Paris instead of escaping to some part of the country where royalist feeling was still strong, even though this might have led to civil war. If the king led his loyal armies and mercenary soldiers against the forces of the assembly, he would soon have been joined by the many aristocrats who had already fled to royalist strongholds or left the country.

Allegations of bribe taking have dogged Danton even after his death. Although many historians agree that he accepted money from special interests, there is little agreement that he allowed these bribes to change his policies.

THE BETTMANN ARCHIVE

Robespierre preparing to drink blood squeezed from a human heart. Verse that accompanied this picture predicted that the ruthless strength he displayed while in power would eventually bring him down. Indeed, Robespierre was guillotined soon after this caricature appeared in 1794.

The first great wave of upper-class emigration began the day after the Bastille fell. These emigré aristocrats were in continual agitation, bitterly hostile to the Revolution, and fiercely loyal to the king. They begged the kings of Spain and Prussia and the emperor of Austria to go to war against what they considered to be a monstrous uprising that had deprived them of their rights, privileges, even their homes. They warned that the Revolution, unless checked, would spread outside France and destroy all aristocrats, kings, and emperors throughout Europe. In the Tuileries, Louis XVI and his trusted advisers secretly kept in close touch with all these "traitors."

The king's fondest hope was that the Constituent Assembly would finish its constitution and go home. Mirabeau, the king's most important ally, assured Louis that new elections would produce a more conservative assembly which could undo the most radical reforms passed by the current representatives. But Mirabeau became ill and died on April 2, 1790. He was buried in the Cathedral of

Sainte-Geneviève, newly renamed "The Panthéon" and made a mausoleum for France's heroes. All Paris mourned his passing, but the king had lost more than the mob. Though Louis rarely followed his champion's advice, he well knew the value of such a devoted and popular defender. With Mirabeau gone, the king suddenly seemed more vulnerable, more like a hostage in his crowded, buzzing palace. Tensions were rising, and came to a head in the Saint-Cloud affair, in which Danton played a major role.

Saint-Cloud is a town just north of Paris where the royal family often spent summers and holidays. Louis decided to take his family there to celebrate Easter in 1791, and Lafayette called out the National Guard to help assure his safe departure from Paris. The troops on duty included members of Danton's old Cordeliers battalion. At Danton's urging, the men of the Cordeliers asked the other battalions to help them prevent the king from leaving Paris. Lafayette, enraged, asked for a declaration of martial law, but Danton pursuaded other members of the city government to refuse his request. Lafayette offered to resign, but Danton shamed him. "Only a coward could desert his post in the hour of peril!" he said. On the day of Louis's scheduled departure the Paris mob shouted insults at Queen Marie-Antoinette and blocked the royal carriages. The National Guard refused to obey Lafayette's orders. There was no longer any doubt: the Tuileries had become a prison.

The Saint-Cloud affair showed Louis XVI exactly where he stood. He realized that if he wanted to escape with his family from the clutches of the Paris mob, he had to be prepared to risk everything, even his life. If the king escaped to join forces with his aristocratic supporters (who were backed by foreign kings), war would almost inevitably follow. This war would be one of neighboring monarchies against the Revolution, and a civil war between supporters of the king and those who wanted to take the Revolution even further. Europe would be changed forever by an escape attempt, but Louis realized that it must be made.

6

Two Fugitives

The king's escape attempt came on the night of June 20, 1791. At 10:15 P.M. a young Swedish officer who was particularly devoted to Marie-Antoinette drove a hired carriage up to a back door of the south wing of the Tuileries Palace. He was dressed as a cab driver. There were so many wild rumors that the king would attempt to flee that Mayor Bailly himself was spending the night in the palace, and all the doors were closely guarded — all but one. Through this unguarded door came the royal family in disguise. The king's brother, the count of Provence, also fled Paris. Louis's youngest brother, Charles Philippe de Bourbon, had foreseen the worst and had fled the country at sunrise the morning after the fall of the Bastille.

After a long day of travel, the king and his family were within miles of friendly troops when a man in the town of Sainte-Ménehould recognized the king by the picture of him which appeared on French currency. The travelers were halted by a local official, a grocer, in the town of Varennes. The Constituent Assembly was duly notified, and deputies were sent to bring the prisoners back.

> *When the people undertake to reason, all is lost.*
> —VOLTAIRE
> 18th-century
> French philosopher

As the Revolution continued Danton's position became steadily more complicated. He had risen to prominence as a spokesman for unemployed Parisians, but other, more radical leaders began to challenge his leadership.

The captured royal family is taken back to Paris from Varennes. Relations between Louis and the people of France deteriorated rapidly after the king's unsuccessful flight from his unruly "subjects."

The wheel of revolution had turned another notch. In Paris, many voices were raised in fear and anger, and Danton's was one of the loudest. In a speech given before the Cordelier Club, which Danton had formed with his supporters in the Cordeliers district, he charged that "By upholding a hereditary monarchy the Constituent Assembly has reduced France to slavery!" He stirred up an excited crowd in the Tuileries gardens by announcing that "Your leaders are traitors! You have been betrayed!" In the usually more sedate Jacobin Club, he and Robespierre both dramatically offered to sacrifice their lives for the Revolution. Danton attacked poor Lafayette, the man responsible for guarding the king, as either a traitor or a fool.

The debate over the form the government should take if the king were deposed was passionate and chaotic. Some put forward the idea of a regency government under Philippe Égalité. Marat even wildly proposed that Danton should be made dictator. (Danton was sensibly horrified. "A fine proposal!" he exclaimed. "Why not have me anointed at Reims?") Meanwhile, the marquis de Bouillé, who had been waiting for the king just beyond Varennes, sent the assembly an emotional letter threatening the representatives — and the city itself — with certain destruction if anything happened to the king and queen.

The Constituent Assembly was torn between the people's rage at Louis's "treachery" and the very real danger of full-scale war with foreign powers if he were deposed. Finally, to protect the king from his fiercest enemies, the assembly guaranteed his personal safety and decided to keep him on his tottering throne as a kind of puppet, a royal prisoner, until he could give his blessing to their new constitution.

Louis XVI as a captive of the Constituent Assembly. After his return to Paris the king was stripped of his power and pressured into accepting the Constitution of 1791.

Women in the forefront of the revolutionary forces invade the assembly. Fearful of foreign invasion and enraged by the king's escape attempt, they demanded the death penalty for members of the aristocracy.

This compromise pleased no one. By the time the Constitution of 1791 was finished (it had taken two and a half years), no one much cared. The assembly could no longer contain the forces of the Revolution. Public outcry demanded that the king be deposed and the monarchy replaced by a republic. If the Constituent Assembly allied itself with the king, the people would overthrow the assembly, too.

The division between the people and their deputies widened tragically on the Champ de Mars, a large field in Paris where the citizens gathered to honor the second anniversary of Bastille Day. Before the day of the celebration arrived, the Cordelier Club, led by Danton, drew up a petition to be circulated among the crowd demanding that Louis be stripped of his crown. Before the petition could be introduced, a delegation of Jacobins arrived at the Champ de Mars to steal the Cordeliers' glory with a stronger petition. The Jacobin petition demanded that the king be brought to trial. The people began to sign their names, and 6,000 signatures were collected.

Suddenly, however, the National Guard arrived in belated response to an ugly incident that had occurred that morning, when two drunks had been murdered. Mayor Bailly and Lafayette arrived hours later with troops to "restore order" to the essentially peaceful celebration. No one knows exactly how it happened, but Lafayette's soldiers fired on the unarmed crowd.

About 50 people were killed and many more were wounded in the "Massacre of the Champ de Mars." Danton was not among the casualties, however; he wasn't on the field. As at the storming of the Bastille and the march to Versailles, Danton was content to avoid the demonstrations spurred by his speeches, keeping himself safe to plan and inspire future battles. In fact, the only Cordelier or Jacobin leader who circulated petitions on the Champ de Mars was Robespierre, who dodged musket bullets on the field and then narrowly escaped being beaten by angry guardsmen. When Danton heard what had happened on the Champ de Mars, he exploded. "If La-

The Bastille Day celebration, which took place in the Champ de Mars on July 17, 1791, ended in tragedy when Lafayette's troops killed approximately 50 unarmed demonstrators. Until then revolutionary factions had united against domination by the monarchy, Church, and aristocracy. Now they were fighting each other.

fayette has fired on the people, he's done for! Those who drink the people's blood die of it."

Danton and his friends had good reason to lay low this time. The same crackdown on the mob that led to the massacre had also produced a warrant for Danton's arrest. He slipped out of Paris and went to stay with Gabrielle's parents in the country. Then Danton decided to flee farther, all the way back to Troyes, where he had gone to school. The long arm of the law threatened the frightened Cordelier even in his home territory. When he was warned that the public prosecutor of Troyes had sent a detachment of soldiers to arrest him, Danton quickly packed for a longer trip, armed himself with pistol and dagger, and made his way to England. It was only four months since this fugitive revolutionary had prevented the king from leaving for Saint-Cloud.

7

The King of the Jacobins

The clear impossibility of the king's position after the unsuccessful flight to Varennes made the appeals of Europe's counterrevolutionary aristocrats more urgent. As the clouds of war gathered, the anticlimactic constitution was finally finished and the Constituent Assembly prepared to go out of business. The weary representatives passed a "Self-Excluding Ordinance" that prohibited their election to the legislative body that would take over after the assembly dissolved. On September 18 the king proclaimed his acceptance of the Constitution of 1791, a carefully-worded document intended to halt the progress of the Revolution and keep power in the hands of the wealthy middle class (the class to which most of the deputies belonged).

The king may have been forced to accept the constitution, but revolutionary Paris was in no mood to do so, especially after blood had been spilled on the Champ de Mars. In a time of external threats and internal conflicts, the departing representatives were leaving plenty of difficult tasks for their successors.

Everything about him is indeed phenomenal, monstrous, in the real sense of the word — his physique, his character and his role.
—HENRI BÉRAUD
French historian,
on Danton

Painting by Gustave Doré representing *La Marseillaise*. This patriotic woman leading a troop of Marseille's citizen soldiers came to symbolize revolutionary feeling in Paris and throughout the country.

Girondin leaders leaving the Revolutionary Tribunal after their fall from power. While in power, the Girondins faced the problem that would eventually destroy both Danton and Robespierre: how to keep order and control the forces of revolution without provoking dissenters into open revolt.

Danton, meanwhile, realized he could not be arrested if elected to the new Legislative Assembly, so he decided to risk returning to Paris. He was welcomed with rejoicing, first at his own Cordelier Club and then by the Jacobins. When a brave National Guardsman came by to arrest the fugitive hero, the guardsman was himself "arrested" by the mob.

Danton's supporters were vocal and active, but they were generally the poorest, least educated, and most volatile citizens of Paris, a fact that may have kept their leader from winning wider support. He lost the election to the Legislative Assembly, and Danton left Paris to join his wife and children in Arcis. He was sick of politics, and decided to concentrate on being a country gentleman. Most of Danton's rivals, including Bailly and Lafayette, were also out of office. Paris was full of new faces.

The Legislative Assembly met for the first time on October 1, 1791. Most of the new deputies were from the same upper-middle-class background as the representatives to the preceding assembly had been.

A little under half of them were moderates, 35% were conservatives, many of whom supported the king, and 17% were Jacobins, who supported more radical reforms. These legislators had their work cut out for them. The departing deputies had left behind a constitution that pleased no one. Furthermore, the Self-Excluding Ordinance passed by the last assembly guaranteed that this new one would have the additional handicap of inexperience. The Legislative Assembly's sessions were notoriously rude and disorderly. As the assembly stumbled, the Paris leaders grew stronger, particularly Maximilien Robespierre.

Danton quickly grew tired of his self-imposed exile in Arcis. He returned to Paris and ran for the office of first deputy public prosecutor. Again, Danton lost; but the king immediately appointed the winner to his cabinet, which made him ineligible for his elected post. (Louis's unusual action suggests that Danton may indeed have been on the king's payroll.) On a second ballot, he finally won the election. Danton made a powerful speech at the swearing-in ceremony, attacking the enemies of France and vowing to uphold the constitution. "I have consecrated my entire life to the people," he said. Paris was now firmly in the hands of Danton in the city government and Robespierre at the Jacobin Club.

The Legislative Assembly, however, belonged to the conservatives, who could usually sway the moderates to their point of view. The conservatives were known as Girondins because their official leader, Jacques-Pierre Brissot de Warville, came from the Gironde region. The Girondins believed that power should be held by the middle class, and were fearful of the masses that their rivals, the Jacobins, appealed to. The group's real leader was the wife of one of the representatives, the beautiful, charming, and keenly intelligent Madame Roland. This dazzling Parisian, married to an older and somewhat plodding civil servant, was chief hostess and major strategist of the party. The Girondins worked hard to achieve their major objective: war.

According to Brissot, France needed war "to consolidate its freedom," "to purge away the vices of despotism," and "to banish from its bosom the men who might corrupt its liberty." The Girondins believed that war would establish the enlightened middle-class republic they longed for. The Girondins also dreamed of exporting the democratic ideals of the Revolution to benefit the common people of other countries.

Few men raised their voices in opposition to the general clamor for war. One who did was Robespierre, insisting at the Jacobin Club that the nation was completely unprepared for a war "contrived by enemies of the Revolution" and that it would be a certain disaster. Another leader who opposed war was Deputy Public Prosecutor Danton, who attacked the supporters of war with such passion that he actually got involved in a fistfight at the town hall with more militant officials.

At Brissot's urging, the assembly sent an ultimatum to the emperor of Austria. If the emperor could not give absolute assurance that he would renounce all other treaties and live in peace with the French people, the assembly would consider his failure to do so the equivalent of a declaration of war. Emperor Leopold II didn't have time to respond to the ultimatum — on March 1, the deadline for his response, the emperor was dead. This unexpected event was taken as a great omen. When the members of the Legislative Assembly voted on their next course of action, only seven men held out for peace. On April 20, 1792, Louis XVI was brought before the assembly to declare war on Austria, his queen's homeland.

Robespierre's prophecy of disaster began to come true almost at once. The war sought so eagerly by these idealistic, inexperienced deputies would last, in one form or another, for over 20 years (almost two decades longer than most of the triumphant Girondist leaders would last themselves). Girondist General Charles-François Dumouriez ordered an invasion of Belgium as the armies of Austria and Prussia prepared to enter France. (Brissot had recently assured the assembly that Prussia would never fight.) When the French troops on the Belgian frontier were thrown back in their first offensive, they murdered an aristocratic general and deserted. Many officers also deserted, some to join the enemy; they were not used to a republican army that voted on whether or not to follow orders. General Rochambeau, France's commander-in-chief (another champion of liberty who had fought in America with Washington), resigned his command.

Although Robespierre had been right when he had predicted that France would fare badly in war, being right doesn't always make a man popular. Robespierre's grim predictions angered the war-hungry people, and his influence began to decline. The Jacobin Club, seeking a new president, turned to Danton. Danton accepted. One of his first acts as president was a speech in praise of the courage and integrity of Robespierre.

In response to the increasingly bad news from the front, the king dismissed the Girondin ministers and appointed new men. This outraged many Parisians and, as usual, their leaders fanned the flames of revolt. Danton, for example, demanded that Marie-Antoinette be sent back to Austria. Lafayette wrote from the front to beg the assembly to take action against "the regime of the clubs." Meanwhile, Danton upset the many wealthy members of the Legislative Assembly by demanding that the rich be taxed proportionately more than the poor to support the war. As the rift between the people and the wealthy representatives widened, a mob of agitated Parisians broke into the Tuileries Palace on June 20. They insulted the queen and forced the king to put on the red liberty cap associated with Jacobin republicanism.

Louis and Marie-Antoinette displayed such bravery in the attack that they won considerable sympathy from their tormentors. Lafayette rushed back to Paris to demand that the assembly put those responsible for these "acts of violence" on trial, and also to repeat his insistence that the representatives "stamp out" the Paris clubs. Typically, Danton stayed out of sight until Lafayette, now the hero of the changeable mob, left again for the front.

The assembly temporarily suspended Mayor Jérôme Pétion and Public Prosecutor Manuel (Danton's boss) for their part in the Tuileries incident. Since Danton had not been directly involved, he kept his job. Once again, Danton had stirred things up, but kept his distance from the trouble.

Meanwhile, the war went on, and it continued to go badly for France. The assembly, the king, and Danton all called for much-needed volunteers. Soldiers from all over France stopped in Paris on their way to the front for the annual Bastille Day celebration. The newcomers included 600 desperate cutthroats from the city of Marseille, who marched into town singing a new revolutionary song, the stirring "Marseillaise," which would eventually become the French national anthem.

The growing movement to depose the king, popular with these republican volunteers and gaining support in every section of Paris, got a big boost when the Brunswick Manifesto was published. The duke of Brunswick was the leader of the Prussian army. On August 1, 1792, he issued a proclamation that promised Paris "utter destruction" and its citizens "the firing squad" if the Tuileries were invaded again.

On August 10, 1792, an angry mob invaded the Tuileries for the second time. Against the queen's wishes, the king took his family to the security of the Legislative Assembly. Those who remained in the palace were massacred.

Louis XVI is threatened by the mob during the first attack on the Tuileries Palace. The irate citizens of Paris terrorized the royal family and forced the king to wear a red cap associated with Jacobin republicanism.

The Girondins who controlled the assembly were in a difficult spot. They hesitated to start the wheel of revolution turning against the king once again, for fear they would not be able to control it once it started — but the Paris mob would not wait. On August 10, volunteers from Marseille and the staunchly republican districts of Paris seized the town hall, suspended the city government, set up a new government (the Insurrectional Paris Commune), and mounted a serious attack on the Tuileries Palace.

Caricature of the increasingly unpopular royal family as farm animals being escorted to the Temple prison. They were moved there after the Tuileries Palace was invaded twice in 1792.

Danton was in the thick of all the plotting. He had urged this attack with passion and eloquence, but, as usual, he had second thoughts about becoming directly involved. On August 6 he left Paris for a visit to Arcis, but Robespierre, Desmoulins, and all his Jacobin colleagues begged him to come back, which he did on August 9, the day before the attack. According to accounts published many years after these events, Danton was deeply involved in the creation of the Insurrectional Commune and in all aspects of the attack on the Tuileries. Danton gave the orders, including one calling for the execution of the uncooperative commander of the National Guard. The day before the attack, Danton announced, "Tomorrow the people will be victorious, or I shall be dead!"

Despite his radical proclamations, Danton also worked to save the lives of the royal family. His actions during this period lend credibility to Lafayette's charge that he was in the pay of the king.

Madame Elisabeth, the king's sister, is said to have told her friends on August 9, "There's no danger. Danton will take care of us."

The king was guarded by 5,000 well-trained soldiers, including tough Swiss mercenaries and dedicated royalist volunteers. But at the first sight of his people in arms (and much against the queen's wishes), Louis ran away, across the gardens, to throw himself and his family on the mercy of the Legislative Assembly. Behind him, a fierce battle took place. Eight hundred died defending the departed king, and nearly 400 republicans were killed in the attack.

As the king and his family sat listening behind a window, the deputies voted to dissolve their assembly. They "suspended" the king for the time being, offered him their protection, and called for new elections. The representatives planned a National Convention, which would solve the difficult problem of what to do with the obsolete monarch. In addition, the deputies agreed to a proposal put forth by Danton that extended the vote to all Frenchmen, even the poorest. If the mob could help elect deputies, maybe it would stop voting with guns and clubs. Before they left office, the deputies appointed new ministers.

Disgusted by the storming of the Tuileries, and unable to rally his men for a march on Paris, Lafayette crossed the border and gave himself up to the Austrians. He spent the next six years in an Austrian dungeon. It was the safest place for him: Lafayette is one of the few revolutionary leaders who survived the Revolution. In Paris he would certainly have been guillotined.

The wheel of revolution had turned another notch away from the king, and was also beginning to move past the Girondins. After the bloody victory of August 10, real power finally flowed to the Jacobins. The assembly, attempting to make peace with the radical opposition and restore order in the government, offered the president of the Jacobin Club and the chief engineer of the attack on the Tuileries a job in the new cabinet. Danton became France's minister of justice.

8

Savior of France

The Girondins thought that of all the Jacobin leaders, Danton was the one man who might actually be able to control the Paris mob. The new minister began his work by giving his friends (Desmoulins, the poet Fabre d'Églantine, and others) jobs in the justice department. Together with his family (Gabrielle had given him another son in February), Danton moved into the Ministry Palace.

Danton tried to make himself agreeable to the Girondins. He even began to attend gatherings organized by Madame Roland. In times of national crisis, or of conflict and indecision in the assembly, it was natural that the power of the ministers, the men who gave orders and made decisions for the day-to-day operation of the government, would increase. As the Legislative Assembly prepared to give way to the new National Convention, the ministers were running the country. Danton's natural authority and vitality, and his popularity, soon made him the dominant minister. He worked feverishly, signing 123 decrees in one eight-day period.

One operation that now fell under Danton's supervision was a special court, the Tribunal of August 17, 1792, set up by the assembly to try those guilty of "crimes against the people" on the day of the Tuileries attack. Dr. Guillotin's machine had made its debut in April 1792 (its first victim was a thief). The new tribunal began sending a trickle of political "criminals" to the scaffold.

> *Like a cyclone he carried everything with him, and upset everything as he passed.*
> —HENRI BÉRAUD
> French historian,
> on Danton

Danton speaking before Paris's Surveillance Committee. As minister of justice, Danton was more powerful than the Girondins with whom he shared the cabinet. Respected by all sides, he could maneuver behind the scenes and still keep his public credibility.

THE BETTMANN ARCHIVE

With the king incarcerated in the Temple prison, Madame Roland persuaded Danton to move cabinet sessions into the vacant Tuileries Palace, to the room where Louis XVI had met with *his* ministers. Danton now sat in the king's chair. Less than 20 years after sneaking into the cathedral at Reims to see Louis XVI crowned, Danton had become a kind of king himself.

France needed a bold, resourceful leader like Danton. The Prussian army (led by the duke of Brunswick, who had threatened Paris with destruction) marched slowly but surely towards the capital. The armies of France fell back as his troops advanced. Some representatives spoke of moving the assembly beyond the Loire River, and Danton even had to reprimand a minister for recommending that Paris be evacuated.

Condemned aristocrats are called to execution. As resentment and paranoia escalated, a trickle of political executions became a flood in 1792. Many other prisoners died without trials at the hands of enraged crowds.

On the very day that the Brunswick Manifesto had appeared in the assembly, a deputy named Lazare Carnot had proposed a new philosophy for France. The whole nation, he said, must become "a nation in arms," with every citizen a soldier. Now, with Brunswick's troops only two weeks from Paris, Danton encouraged his countrymen to embrace Carnot's ideals. He began by rallying volunteers for the front. On August 23, 1792, the Prussians won a major victory and took the city of Longwy, "but Longwy is not France," exclaimed Danton. "It is time to tell the people that they must fling themselves against the enemy. . . . When our country is in danger, it has first claim on everything!" He ordered the confiscation of all arms and any materials that would be helpful in the war effort.

In the midst of the general confusion and outbreaks of panic Danton was everywhere at once, rallying the people and directing their energies. On September 1, 1792, as the enemy continued to approach, Danton exclaimed, "Part of the people will guard our frontiers; part will dig trenches; and still others will defend our towns with pick-axes." The next day, Parisians could hear the thundering of Prussian guns as the nearby city of Verdun fell to the enemy. But Brunswick was slow to advance and Danton was magnificent in the crisis. "The bell you will hear today," he told the people, "is not an alarm, but an alert! It sounds the charge against the enemies of our country. For victory we must be bold, and bold again—forever bold!"

In this moment of great fear and excitement, one of the most shameful and tragic episodes of the Revolution took place. The Paris mob, continually stirred up by its leaders, finally responded to the threat from abroad by attacking "enemies" at home. The prisons of Paris were filled — with Swiss soldiers who had survived their heroic defense of the Tuileries, with nobles and supporters of the king, with priests and nuns hostile to the Revolution, and with many others suspected for one reason or another (a careless remark, a gossipy neighbor) of being "enemies of France." If the Parisians had to face the Prussian soldiers as "a nation in arms," they were

The department of justice fell to Danton, who . . . now no longer wished to serve anything save his own ambition. He was to move towards dictatorship along with Marat and Robespierre. The choosing of Danton was the ruin of France.
—CHARLES-JEAN-MARIE BARBAROUX
Girondist politician, on Danton's appointment as minister of justice

On September 20, 1792, the nation's morale soared after French troops unexpectedly triumphed over Prussian forces at the battle of Valmy. "We have lost far more than a battle," said a Prussian general after the defeat.

determined to leave no "traitors" or "conspirators" alive in Paris. So, on the day Verdun fell, 20 "traitorous" priests being transported to prison were dragged out of their carriages and murdered by the mob. For the next two days, the mob, drunk with blood, attacked various prisons and massacred prisoners. Among the "enemies" slaughtered in these attacks were such nonpolitical victims as 35 prostitutes at the Saltpetrière prison and over 150 children in the reformatory at the Bicêtre jail.

The authorities responsible for protecting these prisoners — Antoine-Joseph Santerre, the popular brewer who was the new head of the National Guard; the deputies; the ministers; the officials of the municipal government — stood idly by and did nothing, or worse, planned and participated in the murders. Jean-Paul Marat had specifically called for lynching prisoners, but even Danton's patriotic speeches had hinted at the need for violence. He told his countrymen, "When a ship is wrecked, the crew throw overboard anything which might place their lives in peril. Similarly, all potential dangers to the nation must be rejected from its bosom." During the prison massacres, Danton washed his hands of responsibility: "Anyone who tried to oppose the justice of the people would be regarded as their enemy," he said.

There is some evidence that he did maneuver behind the scenes to save certain prisoners. Perhaps he could also take credit for keeping Robespierre from putting some leading Girondins, including Minister Roland, on the list of victims. There is also some evidence that Danton himself ordered some of the massacres.

At different times, to different witnesses, Danton both denied and admitted responsibility for the September massacres. Danton may have been capable of ordering the attacks, but he was also capable of claiming "credit" for them falsely. In truth, most Parisian leaders shared responsibility for the cruel slaughter of unarmed prisoners. There were around 2,800 prisoners in Paris at the time. 1,335 were spared by swift "trials"; the rest were massacred by the mob.

As the Prussians threatened the capital and Parisians continued their rampage, the nation was holding elections for the National Convention, which was being called to replace the now unpopular war-mongering Legislative Assembly and to decide the fate of the king. Danton's days of losing elections were over. The energetic minister was the first choice of the Paris electorate. His friend Desmoulins was second, and Robespierre was third. The Parisians also sent Marat to the National Convention. The first meeting of the new legislative body took place on September 20, 1792. On the same day, the armies of France, swollen with volunteers recruited by Danton, and under the command of the bold General Dumouriez, met the Prussians at Valmy and won a decisive victory. The long march of the enemy was over. Paris, for now, was safe.

There may have been more to this victory than the excellent leadership of Dumouriez and the splendid morale of the "nation in arms." Danton may have played a crucial, though secret, role in the French triumph at Valmy. Leaving most of the affairs of his justice department to his underlings (especially Desmoulins), Danton labored to keep England and Spain out of the war, offered Austria peace and a secret alliance, tried repeatedly to pacify

> *In spite of his faults and errors, we must not forget that once, when all appeared lost, he saved France and, remembering that, we should be indulgent.*
> —HENRI BÉRAUD
> French historian,
> on Danton

CULVER PICTURES

The monarchy was abolished and the first French Republic was officially inaugurated on September 21, 1792. While France celebrated the opening days of the Republic the leaders of the new government prepared to face dissension at home and war abroad.

Prussia, and may finally have succeeded in bribing the Prussian commander, the much-hated duke of Brunswick. All this diplomacy was kept secret, as the assembly continued to be uncompromisingly militant.

The factors behind the Prussian defeat at Valmy remain one of the biggest mysteries of the French Revolution. As Brunswick was already a very rich man, it would have taken more than money to buy him. Danton may have been in a position to offer a more unique prize.

The duke of Brunswick had a well-known passion for precious stones. His collection was famous all over Europe. On four evenings in September a series of suspicious robberies took place at the National Archives building in Paris. The loot included the Crown Jewels of France. When the thefts were discovered, Interior Minister Roland immediately (and most unusually) took over the investigation himself. The team of thieves involved — a group of about 50 men — had more or less walked out of La Force prison (which was under the direct authority of Minister of Justice Danton), put a ladder up to the unguarded window at the archives, taken as many valuables as they could carry, and — unbelievably — come back on three different nights for more. Most of the larger treasures were soon recovered, but Roland's men could not find one famous stone, which was known as the Blue Diamond of the Golden Fleece.

General Dumouriez and the duke of Brunswick, though opponents on the field, were personal friends. They both belonged to a secret society called the Masons, which professed enlightened, liberal ideas, and practiced elaborate, mysterious rites. Danton was a Mason, too, as was Carra, the man sent on a mission to Dumouriez just after the Blue Diamond was stolen. Carra had a connection to Brunswick, too. He was such a strong supporter of the duke that he had publicly promoted him (before the duke issued the hated Brunswick Manifesto) as a model king. Carra was the perfect man to deliver a special present to the Prussian general from the wily Danton.

Just before the decisive battle of Valmy, Brunswick had failed to take advantage of an obvious strategic mistake by Dumouriez and attack and crush the French army. Why?

At Valmy, after the two sides exchanged heavy artillery fire, Brunswick decided not to send his army into battle and ordered a retreat instead. Why?

Did Danton buy a crucial victory with a famous diamond?

The Blue Diamond of the Golden Fleece did turn up, eventually. It had been cut, and the larger piece was found in the duke of Brunswick's collection when he died in 1806. The smaller piece, a 40-carat stone, went to England, where it became part of the crown of King George IV. It had been brought to him by his bride, Caroline of Brunswick, the duke's daughter, as part of her dowry. (When George and Caroline agreed to separate, she took back her diamond. Many years later it was purchased by a rich American named Hope, and the Hope Diamond — as this little piece of French and English history is now called — can currently be seen at the Smithsonian Institution in Washington, D.C.)

The long chain of circumstantial evidence indicates that Danton decided France needed a military victory more than a diamond.

The triumph at Valmy, however it was achieved, allowed the National Convention to give its attention to its most pressing domestic problem — the fate of the monarchy. On September 21, 1792, the day after Brunswick's retreat began, the convention voted to abolish royalty. France was officially a republic.

There was not much else the deputies could agree on, and the National Convention split into hostile parties. The debates, which were sharp and bitter from the beginning, would eventually lead to bloodshed and the Reign of Terror. The Girondins were once again in the majority; the Jacobins were their increasingly powerful opposition.

After Valmy the nation became enthusiastic about the war once again. New confidence produced new victories, and General Dumouriez returned to Paris a great hero. Around this time, the convention

The splendid Hope Diamond is part of one of the greatest mysteries that surround the French Revolution. Many historians believe that Danton used the huge stone the Hope Diamond was cut from to buy the crucial French military victory at Valmy.

THE BETTMANN ARCHIVE

79

forced Danton to choose between his ministry post and his new deputy's seat. Although his public speeches and private strategies had played a great part in securing France's military successes, he still found the prospect of wider war unappealing. Rather than continue to direct policies he didn't entirely support, and perhaps preferring to put his particular talents on display in the great public arena of the convention, he resigned from the cabinet and took his seat in the National Convention.

The deputies turned to their unfinished business with the king and voted to put him on trial. On November 20 a locksmith came forward with a story that helped seal the king's fate. The man said that he had built Louis a secret safe in the Tuileries Palace. Afterwards, the locksmith almost died of a sudden, unexplained illness. Believing that he had been poisoned to insure his silence, his revenge was to

Mass killings were common during the Reign of Terror, imposed on France in 1793 by Robespierre and the Jacobins. Danton sometimes praised, sometimes condemned this rough "justice" and tried hard to keep his distance from the violence.

reveal his secret now that the king had become so vulnerable. Interior Minister Roland opened the safe before he revealed its existence to the convention. Inside he found all sorts of incriminating letters and receipts: a whole history of the king's involvement in counterrevolutionary plots and projects. No evidence was found linking Danton with Louis, but if Roland and Danton had been involved in the theft at the National Archives, Roland might very well have kept such highly incriminating evidence to himself.

As might have been expected, Danton did his best to miss the king's trial. Conveniently, the convention found it necessary to send a commission to Belgium to investigate an ongoing problem with army supplies, and Danton volunteered to go. Urging his fellow deputies to resolve the case quickly, he left for the front.

Danton returned to Paris before the king's fate had been decided. Since he had managed to miss most of the trial, he certainly should not have voted on the verdict. Yet when he saw that nothing could save the king, he realized that to abstain, however pure his motives, would be regarded as either cowardice or downright treachery. Moreover, one of the king's former ministers sent Danton a blackmailing letter, claiming that he would reveal evidence of Danton's bribe taking if Danton did not save Louis. Enraged, Danton reprimanded the convention for its slowness, insisted that a simple majority should be enough to decide the king's fate, pressed for a vote, and, on January 16, 1793, voted with the majority for the king's death.

The guillotine was set up at the Place de la Révolution, and five days later, after bidding his people farewell, the deposed and humiliated Louis XVI was laid on the wooden plank. The former king of France died bravely. "I forgive the perpetrators of my death," he said, "and I pray God that my blood will not fall upon France." His head and body were buried in a grave that was (by special decree) 12 feet deep. The nervous deputies needed a deep grave. They were attempting to bury a man, and a monarchy as well.

This antirevolutionary cartoon shows King Louis XVI as Christ being crucified by rebels while Queen Marie-Antoinette weeps at his side. When it became clear that Danton could not save the king's life, he voted with the majority for Louis's execution.

9

The Wars of the Deputies

The wheel of revolution, set in motion four years earlier when Louis summoned the Estates General, had made a full turn by 1793, but it had not come to a stop. After the king's death the wheel began to move a little faster, and it was now attached to a fatal machine. The blade of the guillotine would rise and fall again and again as the French Revolution progressed.

Danton announced to the convention that the king's head was "a gauntlet" France had thrown down as a challenge to the other kings of Europe. The Girondins, as usual, were dreaming of glorious war. (Brissot spoke of setting "all Europe ablaze.") The National Convention had issued a decree that promised "brotherly assistance" to all rebels everywhere and had already alarmed France's neighbors. The execution of the king increased that alarm.

In this militant atmosphere, Danton realized that wider war was unavoidable. He threw himself into the debate with his usual enthusiasm. "France's boundaries have been marked out by nature," he proclaimed. "We shall expand to meet them on all sides — to the ocean, the Rhine, the Alps, and the Pyrenees."

> *What do I care about my own reputation? Let France be free and my name dishonored.*
> —GEORGES JACQUES DANTON

Opponents of the Revolution are thrown to their deaths. Violence escalated sharply as the people Danton and other leaders had stirred to action began to administer their own brand of justice.

THE BETTMANN ARCHIVE

The arrest of a peasant royalist is carried out by fellow citizens. Denunciation by a single "loyal citizen" could mean death for a suspect.

The representatives decided that the time for negotiations was past. On February 1, 1793, the convention voted to declare war on England and Holland; on March 7, war was also declared on Spain. The great goal of Girondin foreign policy was achieved.

While Danton travelled through Belgium to consolidate France's position there, Gabrielle died giving birth to their fourth son. Danton was grief-stricken when he returned home and heard the news. According to some reports, he insisted that Gabrielle's body be exhumed so he could bid her a last farewell. A few weeks later, however, Danton was back to work and on his way to Belgium once again.

In these dark days, the National Convention was not content to make war on foreign foes alone. The deputies continued to attack one another. Soon after the convention's opening session a Girondin deputy, the novelist Louvet de Couvray, denounced Robespierre for his "dictatorial ambitions" and demanded that he be put on trial. Louvet also shouted a similar provocation at Danton: "You're not king yet, Danton! You enjoy no special privileges here!"

Minister Roland wrote secretly to Dumouriez asking the general's help in overthrowing his old allies, Danton and the Jacobins; later on a Jacobin delegation arrived to ask for Dumouriez's support in establishing a Jacobin dictatorship. Disgusted with the bickering and treachery of the representatives to the National Convention, the general tried to muster his troops to march on Paris. When the soldiers refused, the disillusioned hero of Valmy deserted to the Austrians.

Everyone seemed to think that the best solution for any difficulty or disagreement was the guillotine. Robespierre wanted the convention to order the execution of any general who lost a battle, and Danton pressed for the formation of a special tribunal "to deal with counterrevolutionaries." The Girondins were violently opposed to the creation of this tribunal — they feared that Danton would use this small judicial committee to siphon power away from the full convention — but they could not prevent it. "Let us be ruthless," Danton urged, "so the people won't have to be!" The people of Paris seemed to agree. The mob surrounded the convention and clamored for the creation of the Revolutionary Tribunal.

The deputies were forced to create their own Frankenstein, a monster that would eventually murder many of them. Danton's repentance came too late. "God and my fellow men forgive me," he said after his fall. "I never meant [the tribunal] to become the scourge of humanity it has. All I wanted was to prevent any recurrence of the September massacres." He hoped that the Revolutionary Tribunal would replace the unpredictable mob as the protector of

If the spring of popular government during peace is virtue, the spring of popular government in rebellion is at once both virtue and terror: virtue, without which terror is fatal; terror, without which virtue is powerless!
—MAXIMILIEN ROBESPIERRE
French revolutionary

the nation from domestic enemies, and believed that the tribunal would help to restore order and calm in Paris. Instead, he learned that he and his fellow deputies had given the party — or the individual — in power a swift and efficient mechanism for sending opponents to the guillotine.

As the Revolutionary Tribunal attacked first one group and then another, it was very difficult to tell who was really in power. Although the Girondins commanded a majority in the convention, their supporters were scattered over the whole country, and as time went on their popularity waned. The disasters of the war — especially the effects of a ruinous English blockade of French ports — had cost the Girondins a great many of their hard-hit middle-class supporters.

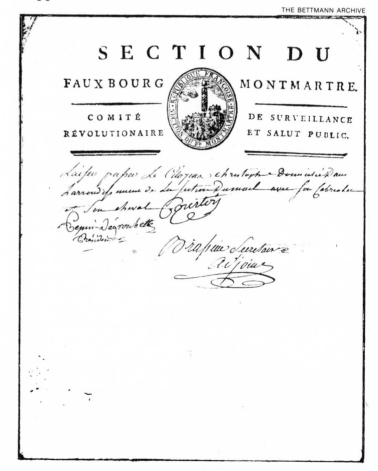

A citizen's passport issued by the infamous Committee of Public Safety. Danton was initially a member of this free-form "justice" organization but was later expelled when his political fortunes declined.

The growing resentment against the Girondin-dominated convention turned into actual rebellion in several parts of France. Fighting had erupted all over the Vendée, a region on the western coast. The support the Girondins had enjoyed throughout the country was reduced by their indecisive response to this revolt, the defeats their armies were suffering on the front, and the desertion of Dumouriez. But the real power in France was not to be found in the provinces, anyway. It was increasingly clear that the Revolution — and the country's future — would belong to whichever party could control the presses, the clubs, and the various districts of Paris. Power had gone to the people, and the people continued to follow the Jacobins.

Marat, the new president of the Jacobin Club, persuaded the convention to form a nine-member Committee of Public Safety to expose "traitors" for the tribunal to bring to trial. The committee was given what amounted to dictatorial powers to run the government. Danton was one of the first nine members, with particular responsibility first in the area of national defense, then in foreign affairs.

Marat's main goal was to overthrow the Girondins. He attacked them as "criminal representatives" and told the mob, "Friends, we are betrayed. To arms!" The Girondins knew they had to move against him. They managed to pass a decree ordering Marat's arrest; but the Revolutionary Tribunal was not about to condemn "the People's Friend." His acquittal doomed the Girondins.

On June 2, 1793, with the Paris government demanding their arrest and the troops of the National Guard posted outside the convention's meeting place to prevent their escape, the Girondin deputies were suspended and arrested by the other members of the National Convention. Minister Roland was one of the few who got away at this time, but Madame Roland did not escape.

France's already chaotic political scene was deteriorating rapidly. As rivalry within the convention threatened to destroy it entirely, the dangers increased. The alliance of foreign enemies of France now included Prussia, Austria, England, Holland,

Danton, the realist, was not attuned to his time; he was lost in a world of idealism.
—HENRI BÉRAUD
French historian

Two peasants from the Vendée fire on revolutionary troops. Many provincials felt betrayed and ignored by the revolutionary presses and clubs of Paris, which seemed to have more power than the National Convention they had elected.

Spain, Portugal, and the states that would eventually become modern Italy. Civil war raged in the Vendée and was spreading throughout the country. A circle of rebellion and peril was being drawn around Paris.

With the removal of the Girondins the convention was finally controlled by the Jacobins, who responded vigorously to the various national crises. They passed harsh decrees and ordered bloody retribution against those involved in local uprisings against the National Convention. Most of the domestic disturbances stopped. The Jacobin policy of executing French generals who lost battles began to produce a tougher army and more victories.

In Paris, equally harsh measures began as the Committee of Public Safety started arresting "enemies" of France and sending them to the Revolutionary Tribunal, which usually sent them on to the guillotine. Ruthlessness, cruelty, and terror became the Jacobin policy for saving France. The Reign of Terror had begun. Behind this policy was the cold, incorruptible idealism of Robespierre, who defined "terror" as "prompt, severe, and inflexible justice."

After Gabrielle died, Danton had thrown himself into his work. He sat on the Committee of Public Safety and on the committee attempting to draw up a new constitution. (The Constitution of 1791 was an embarrassment, since the deputies had executed the man it described as the inviolable head of the government.) Danton frequently spoke before the National Convention — to rally the other deputies, to denounce his enemies and the enemies of France, and to defend himself. The embattled Girondins had

Believing she was avenging the Girondins, Charlotte Corday stabbed the radical Marat to death while he was bathing. Executed for the deed, she died the composed death of a martyr to her cause, but her action sealed the fate of the imprisoned Girondin leaders.

turned their backs on his friendship by bringing up all the old bribery charges. But he did not play a major part in the attack on the Girondins led by Marat and Robespierre. As the persecutions continued, he began to miss convention meetings and to let his responsibilities slide.

Perhaps Danton was tired. Perhaps he was depressed by the way things were turning out: the cannibalism of this convention was a long way from the glorious dreams the young "Republican" had envisioned for France. And perhaps his heart was no longer in his work only because it was somewhere else.

Before she died, Gabrielle had grown very close to her young neighbor, Louise Gély, and Louise had come to think of Gabrielle's children as her own. Danton was, in a sense, fulfilling Gabrielle's plans by falling in love with the 15-year-old girl. On June 17, 1793, Danton married for the second time. It was soon clear to all that the 33-year-old bridegroom preferred wedded bliss to public duties. In July the convention voted to remove him from the increasingly powerful Committee of Public Safety.

With Danton temporarily out of the picture, the plotting and bloodshed continued. A brave young noblewoman from Caen, Charlotte Corday, came to Paris on July 13, 1793, to avenge the Girondin leaders, who were still imprisoned. After stopping off to buy herself a knife, she hired a cab and paid a visit to the man she blamed for the fall of her heroes.

When she arrived, Jean-Paul Marat, the scourge of the Girondins, was sitting in his bathtub, writing. He suffered from a painful skin disease and spent a lot of time in a warm bath. Corday was allowed to see him after she claimed to have information about the political situation in Caen. He asked her for the names of local Girondin leaders and promised her they would all soon face the guillotine. As these thoughts of Girondin bloodshed filled his head, it was Jacobin blood that suddenly filled his bath. Corday killed Marat with her new knife.

Four days later, proud and unafraid, she went to her death. "I am at peace and delightfully content,"

The Girondins approach the guillotine. During the Reign of Terror it was dangerous to appear less than thoroughly revolutionary; the moderate Girondins did not meet the rigorous Jacobin standards of revolutionary purity.

she had written a friend. When the merciful executioner tried to block her view of the guillotine, she objected: "I have the right to be curious," she said, "I've never seen one before."

Marat was hailed as a heroic martyr. The people grieved for their "friend," and grief turned to rage. The assassination was the perfect excuse the Jacobins needed to move against the Girondins. The

The aristocratic Madame Roland is mocked by unsympathetic prison mates during her incarceration. As she approached the scaffold she saw a statue symbolizing liberty beside the guillotine and exclaimed, "Oh Liberty, what crimes are committed in your name!"

Jacobin-controlled convention began by passing a number of harsh decrees, increasing police surveillance and control in the provinces and purging the army of officers sympathetic to Girondin ideals. Finally, the imprisoned Girondin leaders were put on trial. The trial was a show, a kind of free-wheeling debate that ended, according to a new convention decree, when the jury decided that it had heard enough. On October 31, 1793, the Girondin leaders were taken in tumbrels to the guillotine. They sang "La Marseillaise" as their carts passed through the crowded streets. Within 30 minutes 22 people were beheaded.

A week after the Girondin leaders were executed, their guiding spirit followed them to the scaffold. Madame Roland died bravely. Her last words were, "Oh Liberty, what crimes are committed in your name!" When her husband heard of her death he left the house where he was hiding, went out into a field, and shot himself.

Queen Marie-Antoinette, gaunt and half-blind from her long imprisonment, her hair turned white, was tried and executed just before the Girondins were beheaded. She faced the guillotine — and the jeering mob — with courage. When the former queen accidentally stepped on the executioner's foot, she apologized. "Forgive me," she said, "I did not do it on purpose."

While Danton was away the executioner kept busy. The astronomer Bailly, first president of the Estates General and former mayor of Paris, was guillotined. General Jean-Nicolas Houchard, who won many military battles for the Republic, was executed for not winning more. Madame du Barry, who had been the mistress of Louis's father, King Louis XV, screamed and wept and pleaded for her life, to no avail. Priests, aristocrats, soldiers, deputies, complainers, "suspects" — even the young women of Verdun who had given flowers to the duke of Brunswick when he conquered their city in 1792 — all fell before the blade of the guillotine.

The man who created the Revolutionary Tribunal typically played no part in the trial and execution of the Girondins. Danton was in the country with his young wife. He spent his time gardening, fishing in the Aube River, and playing with his children. Danton forbade anyone to bring a newspaper into the house. When neighbors came running with news of the fate of the Girondins, it is reported that he wept. Perhaps Danton believed he was finished with the Revolution, but the Revolution was not finished with him yet.

10

"My Address Will Soon Be Nowhere"

In November 1793 Danton's retreat in the country was interrupted by an urgent message from Paris. Desmoulins and the other "Dantonists" begged him to come back; the power that had destroyed the Girondins would soon be turned against Danton and his followers. Danton had to boldly answer all the rumors about him, especially those that implied he had taken bribes and conspired with enemies of the Republic. Only the old, roguish Danton, making the spectators laugh as he defended himself and attacked his opponents in his big voice, would be strong enough to stand against the increasingly powerful Robespierre.

The National Convention had elected "the Incorruptible" to the Committee of Public Safety, which now openly ruled France. Because of his fame, ruthlessness, and unwavering fidelity to revolutionary principles, Robespierre soon controlled the committee. "Go and tell Robespierre that I'll be there in plenty of time to crush him," Danton told the messenger who informed him of the recent events in Paris, "and his accomplices with him!"

I shall break that damned guillotine before long, or I shall fall under it.
—GEORGES JACQUES DANTON
in 1794

Danton defends himself before the Revolutionary Tribunal in 1794, a year after he helped create the organization. The tribunal, guided by rumor and the power struggles of the time, was a dangerous political forum, as both Danton and Robespierre discovered.

THE BETTMANN ARCHIVE

Danton (right) and his devoted friend Camille Desmoulins at the Luxembourg prison, where they were held immediately after their arrest. Danton spent his last days comforting Desmoulins, who was convinced — correctly — that their executions would not be the last in the Reign of Terror.

When Danton returned to Paris he found the National Convention greatly changed. The leading Girondins were dead, and those deputies who sympathized with them were in prison. Some representatives had arranged to go on missions, like Danton's trip to Belgium, in order to escape Robespierre's purges. Others had just stopped coming to such a dangerous place. Only about half of the 760 elected representatives now attended the sessions.

It is remarkable that an assembly under the constant threat of violence managed to achieve so much, but the deputies of this bloody convention had a passion for making laws as well as for murdering each other. Their numerous decrees covered everything from the establishment of the metric system to the creation of the Louvre Museum. The National Convention's nonviolent labors founded modern France.

Danton took his place among the representatives with his old energy. He called for a French revival of the old Greek custom of olympic games. He demanded compulsory education. But his chief goal was to restore a measure of sanity to the government by bringing the Reign of Terror to an end.

Even Danton was not strong enough to achieve this goal. The deputies, frightened of Robespierre's committee, shouted down any hint of "mercy" for the "enemies" of France. There was great danger, of course, in trying to stop the machinery of the Committee of Public Safety. The committee and its allies — a network of Vigilance Committees and Popular Societies set up to spy, purge, censor, and spread propaganda all over the country; the Committee of General Security (which did the arresting); the Revolutionary Tribunal; and the guillotine — ruled France. Danton attacked this monster of "justice," but he was not able to kill it. Instead, he drew its attention.

Robespierre was not yet ready to strike at Danton. Other, more troublesome rivals had to be dealt with first — the new leaders of the Paris mob. The men who had formerly dominated the mob — Danton, Robespierre, and Desmoulins — lost touch with it, to some extent, when power brought them greater responsibilities and wider support. The Committee of Public Safety had been created to keep the mob both happy and under control, but no government could hope to solve all the problems of the poor. The Paris mob — which had stormed the Bastille and kidnapped the king in 1789, attacked the Tuileries and massacred prisoners in 1792, demanded the arrest of the Girondin deputies in 1793, and shouted their approval each time the blade of the guillotine fell — had found itself new leaders.

Robespierre distrusted a group of fanatic Jacobins known as the Enragés (the Enraged), led by a radical former priest named Jacques Roux. Roux had taken up the cause of the working poor. Increased liberty had not lifted the economic burdens of the poor, and they were ready to rise again and massacre the "enemies" they felt were responsible for their poverty.

The kind colossus loved to love. He never abandoned his friends. Hatred was foreign to his nature; he did not need it.
—HENRI BÉRAUD
French historian,
on Danton

Another enemy of Robespierre was Jacques-René Hébert, a journalist and deputy public prosecutor, who had become the real leader of the city government. Hébert's paper, *Le Père Duchesne*, was even more violent and unprincipled than Marat's newspaper had been. (Hébert, for example, accused Marie-Antoinette of sexual misconduct with her young son.) His paper had a large circulation of up to 600,000 readers. Earlier, Hébert had encouraged his supporters to surround the National Convention and played a big part in toppling the Girondins.

The Enragés and the Hébertists were natural allies, and the Jacobin government their natural enemy. It seemed that once a group was swept into power, the people immediately began to distrust their new leaders, who could never be radical enough to please the Paris mob.

Although Hébert had been critical of Danton in the past, he now sought to form an alliance against Robespierre. This sort of intrigue usually delighted Danton, but this time he refused: Hébert was too contemptible. After Danton rejected an alliance with the Hébertists and continued to support Robespierre, Robespierre defended him at the Jacobin Club, remarking that Danton "has always, to the best of my knowledge, served France with devoted zeal."

At Danton's urging, Desmoulins began publishing a journal whose title, *The Old Cordelier*, was calculated to remind Parisians of better times. (The current president of the Cordelier Club was Hébert.) Danton hoped that Desmoulins's eloquence would promote the new Dantonist policy of moderation and an end to the Terror. Desmoulins was careful to placate his old ally Robespierre by attacking Hébert; but the main purpose of his journal was to change the public mood and inspire a popular demand for an end to the seemingly endless bloodshed. Danton pushed the same policy in the National Convention. The crusade had wide appeal. Danton seemed to be reaching out to all the surviving enemies of the Reign of Terror and Robespierre's severity.

If you save Danton you save a personality — something you have known and admired; you pay respect to individual talent, but you ruin the attempt in which you have so nearly succeeded.
—LOUIS-ANTOINE-LÉON DE SAINT-JUST
Jacobin politician and revolutionary, addressing the Committee for Public Safety

There is some evidence that Robespierre intended to end the Terror himself, when good news from the front would enable him to announce that the country was saved and the need for extraordinary measures had passed. As Danton continued to plead for tolerance, Robespierre thought that he was trying to interfere with his plans and steal the people's gratitude for himself. Danton would have to be dealt with, of course, but not yet.

Sure of his place in history, Danton approaches the guillotine. His efforts to moderate the violence and political persecution carried out in the name of justice brought about his downfall, though he was formally charged with personal misconduct and treason.

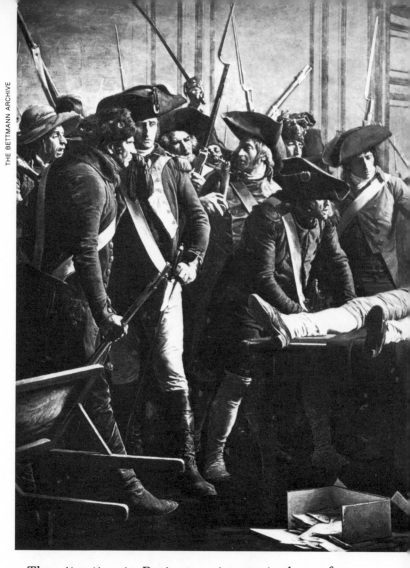

THE BETTMANN ARCHIVE

The situation in Paris grew increasingly confusing and dangerous. France's leaders were playing a complicated game. The winners would get power and glory; the losers would get the guillotine. Desmoulins denounced Hébert, which pleased Robespierre; but he also attacked members of Robespierre's bloodthirsty committee in his newspaper. Robespierre said Desmoulins's newspaper should be seized and burned. Danton sided with Robespierre against Hébert, but stood behind Desmoulins and *The Old Cordelier*. Meanwhile, Hébert and his friends, confident the Paris mob would support them in any crisis, plotted against almost everyone. Jacques Roux, the Enragé leader, was out of

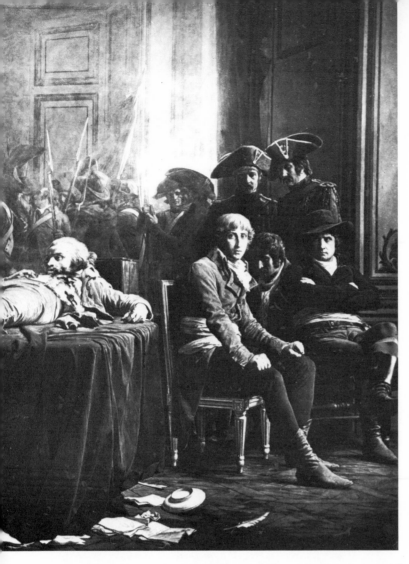

Robespierre lies bleeding on the same table he used to sign Danton's death warrant in his former office at the Committee of Public Safety. After the tide of revolution turned against the Jacobin leader he unsuccessfully tried to cheat the executioner by shooting himself in the jaw.

the game first: he killed himself in prison to avoid a trial conducted by Robespierre's supporters. Hébert was the next to fall. In February 1794 he was executed after an unsuccessful attempt to wrest power away from the Jacobins.

The Enragé and Hébertist leaders had lost and were out of the game. Now, finally, the two great rivals, Danton and Robespierre, faced each other across the bloody chessboard of Revolutionary politics. Danton moved first — to make peace. Robespierre received him coldly. A second meeting ended in an embrace. Reassured, Danton decided to leave Paris at this critical moment and take his family on a country holiday.

Perhaps Danton really thought that embrace ended the "wars of the deputies," that the Reign of Terror would end. Perhaps he thought he could afford to relax because his wit, nerve, and popularity would always save him. Perhaps he was just exhausted and depressed by the violence. "Better, a hundred times better to suffer the guillotine," he said, "than to inflict it on others."

His friends came to tell him he was in danger, but he thought he was more than a match for Robespierre. They urged him to leave France. "Can a man take his country with him on the soles of his feet?" he asked. Nevertheless, after a week's holiday, he returned to Paris.

Danton would have been more than a match for Robespierre — if the combat had been a physical one. But in this political duel to the death Robespierre had the best weapon: the Committee of Public Safety — the machinery Danton himself had helped to create — which made it easy for the man who controlled it to arrest, try, and execute his enemies. For Robespierre's committee, Danton had become the enemy.

A friend of Danton's, a clerk for the Revolutionary Tribunal, overheard the Jacobin leader's plans. He warned Danton that the following day Robespierre's chief supporter, the proud, handsome, implacable Louis-Antoine-Léon de Saint-Just, would ask the convention to approve the arrest and trial of Danton. "They will not dare — they will not dare," Danton muttered when he heard the news.

They dared. The arrest warrant was drawn up and signed. Two more friends came to warn him. "I can't believe it," he said. When the officers came for him on March 31, 1794, Danton went quietly. He told his wife Louise he would be back soon.

Why didn't he flee? Why had he gone to the country and left the field to Robespierre and his allies? Danton's words and actions in those perilous days were those of a man in a dream, not a daring leader. He seemed to passively entrust himself to fate. It was as if he knew the wheel of revolution, which he had spun himself, now had a momentum all its own.

At his trial, however, some of Danton's old spirit returned. In response to the bribery charges against him, Danton thundered, "I sell myself? Men such as I cannot be bought, for upon our foreheads is stamped in indelible characters the seal of liberty, of the Republic." He transformed his trial into an heroic battle and attempted to turn the tables on Robespierre by putting the government itself on trial, hoping to win the sympathies of the deputies and the public as he had done so many times before. The Revolutionary Tribunal had acquitted Marat. Surely the people knew they had a better "friend" in Danton. Surely they would not allow him to be convicted as a traitor to his nation.

On the day following his arrest Danton was defended in the convention, but when Robespierre appeared the intimidated deputies fell silent. Saint-Just rose to read the list of charges the jealous Robespierre had drawn up against his old friend: Danton was accused of being corrupt, a royalist, and a traitor long in league with the enemies of France. Saint-Just maintained that Danton sympathized with the Girondins and advocated a policy of "mercy" that would weaken and destroy the Republic. Witnesses commented on the eerie chopping gesture with which Saint-Just punctuated his two-hour report. At the end, the "Angel of Death" warned the deputies: "The days of crime are ended: woe to those who support such a cause." The intimidated National Convention unanimously approved the charges.

The trial of Danton and his supporters began on April 2, 1794. For the nervous officials of the Revolutionary Tribunal, who knew very well the verdict they were expected to reach, it was a formality full of danger. Perhaps out of bravery, perhaps because they knew they were doomed, the defendants felt free to speak out. They attacked their accusers, made passionate speeches, and interrupted the court. "Didn't you hear my bell?" asked the president of the tribunal after a particularly chaotic exchange. "A man fighting for his life pays no attention to bells!" Danton replied. "He just shouts!"

> *He was a man ready to sell himself to all parties.*
> —MARQUIS DE LAFAYETTE
> French soldier and revolutionary, on Danton

Robespierre awaits execution as the heads of his allies are displayed to the crowd in the grisly ritual of death that became commonplace during the Reign of Terror. The death of Danton's greatest enemy brought the Terror to an appropriately bloody end.

For the Dantonists the trial was a show, a demonstration meant to confound the court and win the sympathies of the people.

The battle lines were clearly drawn from the beginning. When formally asked his name and address, Danton made a famous reply: "My address will soon be nowhere; as for my name, you will find it in the pantheon of history. . . . The people will revere my head when the guillotine has severed it from my shoulders." After he was asked his age, Desmoulins said he was 33 years old, "a dangerous age for revolutionaries" — the same age at which another champion of the common man, Jesus, had been executed. General Westermann, who had led the attack on the Tuileries that had toppled the king, caused a great stir. "I demand permission to strip myself naked before the people and let them see my scars. I have received seven wounds, all of them in front. Only once have I been stabbed in the back — by this indictment!" Danton talked himself hoarse on the second day, but he was not allowed to speak again.

The prosecutor, frightened by the growing public support for the prisoners, became desperate. He had appealed to the Committee of Public Safety, which told the National Convention that it had uncovered a plot, led by Desmoulins's beautiful wife Lucile, to free the prisoners. Faced with such a dangerous situation, the convention agreed to pass a harsh decree stating that "any prisoner who resists or insults the national justice shall at once be debarred from pleading his case."

When Danton was informed of this cowardly decree, he rejected it with contempt. He would not be silent: "I am Danton until I die. Tomorrow I am sure fame awaits me in death!" The others joined him in vigorous protest, and they were escorted out of the court along with their enraged leader. The next day, the prosecutor announced that no witnesses would be called. The jury said it had heard enough. The trial was over. Robespierre could not risk letting Danton speak again.

That night the executioner came to cut their hair, and on the following afternoon, April 5, 1794, three red carts picked the prisoners up at the gates of the Conciergerie prison. They passed the Café de l'École, where the young law clerk had met his first wife. The poet Fabre d'Églantine lamented that he would die without finishing the play he was writing. "Verses!" Danton laughed at him. "In a week you'll be making worms, not verses." They passed Danton's old friend, now Robespierre's crony, the artist Jacques-Louis David, who made a famous last sketch of Danton as he had of Marie-Antoinette. As the carts rolled along, a former monk named Chabot screamed in pain. He had managed to take arsenic in prison and was lifted unconscious to the guillotine. Desmoulins wept, Westermann swore. Danton stared up at the drawn blinds as they passed the modest apartments where Robespierre lived, and shouted, "You will follow me." Finally, the doomed prisoners arrived at the Place de la Révolution.

A monument to Danton, a man who stirred the emotions of the people of France and ultimately fell victim to the passions he unleashed. Although much about his life and motivations remains a mystery, Danton is one of history's most compelling figures.

Hérault de Séchelles, the aristocratic lawyer who had stormed the Bastille and had been president of the National Convention, passed Danton on his way to the scaffold. He leaned forward to kiss his old friend goodbye, but the executioner pulled him away. "Do you think you can keep our heads from kissing in the basket?" Danton asked.

Danton was the last to die. The 34-year-old revolutionary went bravely, reminding the executioner to show his head to the people.

Danton was right about one thing. Robespierre did follow him to the scaffold. Less than four months after the Dantonists were guillotined, the surviving deputies turned on the master of the Terror. Robespierre raged and manipulated and plotted frantically to save himself, but to no avail. His goal had been noble: to create a Jacobin republic, which would give the people of France "the peaceful enjoyment of liberty and equality, and the reign of eternal justice." His means had been less noble: the horrible excesses of the Reign of Terror.

The Republic for which Danton, Robespierre, and so many others lived and died had a profound influence on the development of representative democracy and the course of Western history, but it did not long survive its leaders. The wheel of revolution continued to turn, and it brought many surprises. One of the bravest and brightest of the Republican generals, a Corsican named Napoleon Bonaparte, who carried the old Girondin war all the way to Egypt and Russia, crowned himself emperor of France in 1804. Ten years later King Louis XVI's brother, the count of Provence, who had managed to get away with his wife on the night of the king's flight to Varennes, ascended the throne as King Louis XVIII. (King Louis XVII, Marie-Antoinette's young son, died suspiciously in a republican prison in 1795.) In 1830 an officer who had escaped to the Austrians with General Dumouriez, the son of Louis-Philippe d'Orléans, became King Louis Philippe. The elderly soldier who helped him get his crown was Danton's old enemy, the marquis de Lafayette.

Although Danton's death foreshadowed the demise of his beloved Republic, his legacy lives on. He inspired the people of France to demand liberty and a voice in their government. Yet, in the end, he was unable to control his countrymen as their voices became shouts and liberty a license to violence. His shortcomings and ultimate defeat notwithstanding, the figure of Georges Jacques Danton towers above the other participants in the tumultuous French Revolution.

He has been labelled as everything from a republican Joan of Arc to a royalist gangster.
—NORMAN HAMPSON
British historian,
on Danton

Further Reading

Belloc, Hilaire. *Danton: A Study.* London: Nisbet & Co., 1928.

Béraud, Henri. *Twelve Portraits of the French Revolution.* Translated by Madeline Boyd. Freeport, N.Y.: Books for Libraries Press, 1968.

Hampson, Norman. *Danton.* London: Gerald Duckworth & Co., 1978.

Johnson, Douglas. *The French Revolution.* New York: G. P. Putnam's Sons, 1970.

Levy, Barbara. *Legacy of Death.* Englewood Cliffs, N.J.: Prentice-Hall, 1973.

Palmer, R. R. *Twelve Who Ruled: A Study of the Committee of Public Safety.* Princeton, N.J.: Princeton University Press, 1941.

Thompson, J. M. *The French Revolution.* New York: Oxford University Press, 1966.

———. *Leaders of the French Revolution.* New York: Harper and Row, 1967.

Chronology

Oct. 26, 1759	Georges Jacques Danton born in Arcis-sur-Aube, France
June 11, 1775	Attends the coronation of Louis XVI
1780	Finishes his studies; moves to Paris and works as a law clerk
Oct. 1784	Obtains a law degree
1787	Purchases the office of counsel to the king's bench
1789	Elected president of the Cordeliers district
May 5, 1789	King Louis XVI convenes the Estates General
July 14, 1789	Paris mob storms the Bastille prison-fortress
Oct. 5–6, 1789	The "Bread March of the Women"; mob brings the king to Paris
July 17, 1791	Massacre of the Champ de Mars
Aug.–Sept. 1791	Danton lives in England to avoid arrest
Dec. 1791	Elected first deputy public prosecutor
April 20, 1792	Louis declares war on Austria; Danton subsequently named president of the Jacobin Club
Aug. 10, 1792	The mob storms the Tuileries; Insurrectional Commune created
Aug. 11, 1792	Danton becomes minister of justice
Sept. 20, 1792	France drives back Prussian soldiers at the Battle of Valmy Danton serves as top Paris deputy to the opening session of the National Convention
Sept. 21, 1792	The National Convention abolishes the monarchy; France becomes a republic
Jan. 21, 1793	King Louis XVI guillotined
Feb.–March 1793	France declares war on England, Holland, and Spain
March 10, 1793	Danton persuades the convention to create the Revolutionary Tribunal
April 1793	Elected to the first Committee of Public Safety
June 2, 1793	Girondin deputies expelled from the National Convention and arrested
July 10, 1793	Danton removed from the Committee of Public Safety
July 13, 1793	Jean-Paul Marat assassinated
Oct.–Nov. 1793	Danton retires with his family to Arcis-sur-Aube
Oct. 31, 1793	Girondin leaders guillotined
March 31, 1794	Danton and his followers arrested
April 5, 1794	Danton guillotined
July 28, 1794	Robespierre guillotined

Index

Age of Reason, The, 25
Aix, 34
American Revolution, 24, 42
Angel of Death *see* Saint-Just, Louis-Antoine-Léon de
Arcis-sur-Aube, 19, 20, 25, 37, 64, 65, 70
Arras, 49
Aube River, 19, 21, 93
Austria, 54, 66, 67, 77, 87
Bailly, Jean-Sylvain, 34, 47, 48, 49, 57, 60, 64, 93
Bastille, 16, 38, 40, 41, 54, 57, 60, 97, 106
Bastille Day, 38, 60, 68
Belgium, 66, 81, 84
Blue Diamond of the Golden Fleece, 78, 79
Bonaparte, Napoleon, 107
Bread March of the Women, 43, 44
Brissot de Warville, Jacques-Pierre, 65, 66, 83
Brunswick, duke of, 68, 74, 75, 78, 79, 93
Brunswick Manifesto, 68, 75, 78
Caen, 90
Café de l'École, 28, 105
Carnot, Lazare, 75
Cathedral of Sainte-Geneviève, 55
Champs de Mars, 60, 63
Charles Philippe de Bourbon, 57
Charpentier, Gabrielle *see* Danton, Gabrielle
Committee of General Security, 97
Committee of Public Safety, 87, 89, 90, 95, 97, 102, 105
Conciergerie prison, 16, 105
Constituent Assembly, 35, 42, 45, 51, 54, 57, 59, 60, 63
Constitution of 1791, 40, 51, 60, 63
Corday, Charlotte, 90
Cordelier Club, 58, 60, 64, 98
Cordeliers, 38, 41, 48, 49, 55
Dante, 27
Danton, Gabrielle (first wife), 28, 29, 37, 49, 53, 61, 73, 84, 89, 90
Danton, Georges Jacques
    arrest, 102
    birth, 19
    bribery charges against, 50, 51, 81, 103
    creates Revolutionary Tribunal, 85
    early years, 21, 22, 23, 24

    education, 21
    execution, 16, 17, 106
    lawyer, 27, 29, 30, 37
    marriage, 29, 90
    member of Committee of Public Safety, 87, 89
    minister of justice, 71, 73, 75
    National Convention delegate, 77, 80, 81, 84, 85
    opposes Reign of Terror, 95, 97, 98, 99
    public prosecutor, 65, 66
    revolutionary, 31, 40, 47, 49, 55, 58, 60, 70, 76
    Robespierre and, 49, 67, 77, 95, 98, 101
    on trial, 51, 103, 104, 105
Danton, Louise (second wife), 90, 102
David, Jacques-Louis, 105
Declaration of Independence, 24, 40
Declaration of the Rights of Man, 40, 42, 44
Defoe, Daniel, 30
Desmoulins, Camille, 38, 45, 70, 73, 77, 95, 97, 98, 100, 104, 105
Desmoulins, Lucile, 105
Dumouriez, Charles-François, 66, 77, 78, 79, 85, 87, 107
Égalité, Philippe *see* Louis-Philippe, duke of Orléans
Egypt, 107
England, 61, 77, 79, 84, 87
Enragés, 97, 98, 101
Estates General, 32, 33, 39, 40, 83
Fabre d'Églantine, Philippe, 73, 105
First Estate, 32
Gély, Louise *see* Danton, Louise
George III, king of England, 24
George IV, king of England, 79
Girondins, 65, 66, 69, 71, 73, 77, 79, 83, 85, 86, 87, 88, 89, 90, 91, 92, 93, 96, 98, 103
Guillotin, Joseph Ignace, 15, 16, 73
Hébert, Jacques-René, 98, 100, 101
Hérault de Séchelles, Marie-Jean, 106
Holland, 84, 87
Hope Diamond *see* Blue Diamond of the Golden Fleece
Houchard, Jean-Nicolas, 93
Huet de Paisy, 28, 29

Insurrectional Paris Commune, 69, 70
Jacobin Club (Jacobins), 49, 50, 58, 60, 64, 65, 66, 67, 71, 79, 85, 87, 88, 91, 98, 101
Jefferson, Thomas, 24, 25
Lafayette, marquis de, 42, 43, 45, 47, 48, 49, 50, 55, 58, 60, 64, 67, 70, 71, 107
Legislative Assembly, 64, 65, 66, 67, 71, 73, 77
Leopold II, emperor of Austria, 66
Loire River, 74
Loménie de Brienne, Étienne-Charles de, 37
Longwy, 75
Louis XV, king of France, 93
Louis XVI, king of France, 23, 31, 32, 33, 34, 35, 40, 44, 45, 53, 54, 55, 57, 59, 60, 63, 65, 66, 67, 71, 74, 80, 81, 83
Louis XVII, king of France, 107
Louis XVIII, king of France, 107
Louis-Philippe, duke of Orléans, 50, 58, 107
Louis Philippe, king of France, 107
Louvet de Couvray, Jean-Baptiste, 85
Louvre Museum, 96
Marat, Jean-Paul, 27, 47, 48, 49, 58, 76, 77, 87, 90, 91, 98, 103
Marie-Antoinette, queen of France, 23, 45, 55, 57, 67, 93, 98, 105, 107
Marseille, 68, 69
"Marseillaise, La," 68, 93
Masons, 78
Massacre of the Champs de Mars, 60
Milton, John, 27
Mirabeau, comte de, 34, 51, 54, 55
National Archives, 78, 81
National Assembly, 33
    see also Constituent Assembly; Estates General
National Convention, 71, 73, 77, 79, 80, 83, 85, 88, 89, 95, 96, 98, 103, 105, 106
National Guard, 47, 55, 60, 70, 76, 87
Necker, Jacques, 40
Old Cordelier, The, 98, 100
Palais Royal, 35, 38
Panthéon, The see Cathedral of Sainte-Geneviève
Paris, 13, 25, 27, 35, 38, 39, 40, 41, 45, 53, 55, 58, 60, 61, 63, 64, 65, 68, 69, 74, 75, 76, 77, 81, 85, 87, 88, 89, 96, 100
People's Friend, The, 47
Père Duchesne, Le, 98
Pétion, Jérôme, 67
Place de la Révolution (Place de la Concorde), 16, 81, 105
Portugal, 88
Prussia, 54, 66, 77, 87
Reign of Terror, 16, 79, 89, 97, 98, 99, 102, 107
Reims, 23
Revolutionary Tribunal, 85, 86, 87, 89, 93, 97, 102, 103
Robespierre, Maximilien, 49, 50, 51, 60, 65, 66, 67, 70, 77, 85, 89, 90, 95, 96, 97, 98, 99, 100, 101, 102, 103, 105, 107
Robinson Crusoe (Defoe), 30
Rousseau, Jean-Jacques, 25, 27
Roux, Jacques, 97, 100
Russia, 107
Saint-Cloud, 55, 61
Saint-Just, Louis-Antoine-Léon de, 102, 103
Sainte-Ménehould, 57
Santerre, Antoine-Joseph, 76
Scotland, 27
Second Estate, 32, 33
Seine River, 27
Self-Excluding Ordinance, 63, 65
September massacres, 76, 77, 85
Shakespeare, William, 27
Spain, 54, 77, 84, 88
Third Estate, 32, 33, 34, 35
Troyes, 21, 23, 61
Tuileries Palace, 45, 47, 53, 54, 55, 57, 67, 68, 69, 70, 71, 73, 74, 75, 80, 97, 104
United States, 24
University of Edinburgh, 27
University of Reims, 27
Valmy, 77, 78, 79
Varennes, 57, 59, 63
Vendée, 87, 88
Verdun, 75, 76, 93
Versailles, 32, 33, 35, 40, 41, 43, 45, 60
Voltaire, 25, 27
Washington, George, 42, 67

Frank Dwyer received his B.A. from New York University and his M.A. in English literature from the State University of New York at Buffalo. He has taught English literature at several New York-area schools, including Marymount College and the State University of New York at Buffalo. He worked as an actor and director in New York professional theater for 15 years. He is also the author of HENRY VIII in the Chelsea House series WORLD LEADERS PAST & PRESENT.

Arthur M. Schlesinger, jr., taught history at Harvard for many years and is currently Albert Schweitzer Professor of the Humanities at City University of New York. He is the author of numerous highly praised works in American history and has twice been awarded the Pulitzer Prize. He served in the White House as special assistant to Presidents Kennedy and Johnson.